Total Modernism

Mass Housing and Urbanism in Soviet Zaporizhzhia

1958–1985

This title is part of the Histories of Ukrainian Architecture programme initiated by DOM publishers in response to Russia's attack on Ukraine's sovereignty on 24 February 2022.

Ця книга є частиною серії Історії архітектури України, започаткованої видавництвом ДОМ у відповідь на російську повномасштабну загарбницьку війну проти української держави, розпочату 24 лютого 2022 року.

Total Modernism
Mass Housing and Urbanism in Soviet Zaporizhzhia
1958–1985

Edited by Pavlo Kravchuk

Pavlo Kravchuk,
Mykhailo Mordovskoi

DOM
publishers

Content

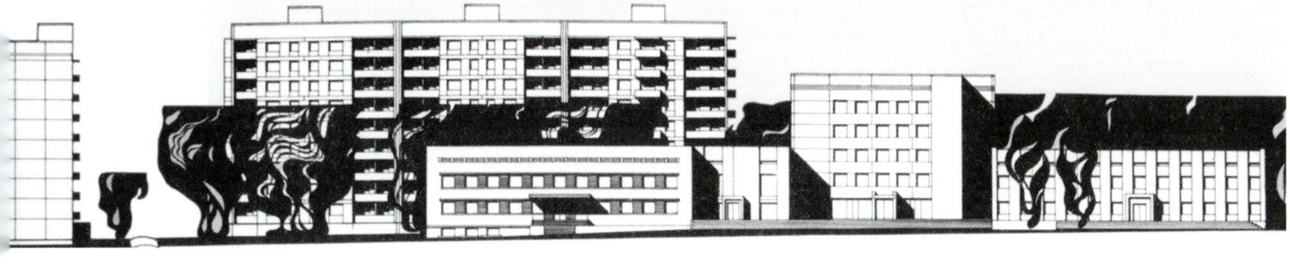

Foreword

This study is a response to the growing confusion in the worldviews of citizens whose personal experience has dissolved beyond recognition in the flux of modernity. Moving during the second half of the twentieth century into housing in Modernist residential areas, the inhabitants of Zaporizhzhia seem to have fallen into a realm of oblivion, their everyday life stuck fast between the past and the future. Deprived of a sense of the flow of history, the space in which they live has turned into a ghetto for individual life stories that fail to come together to form a coherent whole. Zaporizhzhia's recent history has increasingly come to resemble a collection of fragments of unfulfilled strategies for personal and public development.

The established way of looking at the past has denied the meaningfulness of the mass and the typical, preventing a view of Zaporizhzhia as a complex urban reality. Modernist housing slowly acquired pejorative connotations, and its historical and cultural worthlessness became a common rhetorical *topos*. Local urban history proved unable to explain the temporal and spatial influences that are characteristic of micro-districts and residential areas: the connection between modernity and its expanded repertoire of interaction that is free from social control; and the gradual replacement of customary cultural types – the producer with the consumer, the flaneur with the passenger.[1]

The main goal of this book has therefore been to help us form a way to understand Zaporizhzhia as a local historical model of the birth of a modern society with cells for individual experience based on the Modernist residential unit.

In the general historical sense the book refers to the transition from departmental and sectoral practices of urban-space management to the development of autonomous municipal policies. In the late 1950s the redistribution of resources intended for housing and communal and socio-cultural construction led to a significant increase in the role of local councils. It is no exaggeration to say that, with all its flaws and advantages, large-scale Modernist development in Ukrainian cities became a manifesto for what local government can do in conditions of rapid urbanisation. The system of departmental settlements and urban blocks, often extraterritorial, that had been typical of the 1930s and the first half of the 1950s was replaced with planning areas whose formation and maintenance were beyond what could be achieved by individual industrial giants, even with the support of subordinate trade unions. Freed from departmental and sectoral limitations, Modernist housing development turned out to be an ideal space for formation of a Soviet consumer society.

1 Micro-district: in Soviet urban planning a primary unit of urban development comprising a complex of houses and services infrastructure connected with and bounded by main transport arteries. Roughly equivalent to the concept of the 'neighbourhood unit' devised by the American urban planner Clarence Perry in the early twentieth century.

The planned scale of urban transformation left no alternative but to build using a Modernist approach. Modernism knew how to manage the transition from the standardised residential cell/apartment to multi-apartment buildings, urban blocks, micro-districts, and even cities. This was a tacit, belated recognition of the provisions of the CIAM's Athens Charter. The typical design solutions of Modernism translated well into the language of industrial house construction, while demonstrating the specific artistic and aesthetic programme of modern architecture. The external expressiveness of the architectural volumes and the compositional completeness of the complexes usually manifested themselves only at scale – in dynamic movement (observer/passenger) along district and city highways. This, though, often came into conflict with the realities of transportation in the newest residential areas and, ultimately, led to mass rejection of 'monotonous' buildings created to a single design. Instead, citizens were able to appreciate the potential for form-shaping illustrated by Soviet Modernism in projects created to one-off designs or modifications of standardised designs. This study presents ten such projects that represent Zaporizhzhian Modernism of the 1960s to1980s with all its cross-influences.

In a bid to portray the societal orientation of Ukrainian architecture of the second half of the twentieth century, we have focused on the connection between planning / volumetric decisions and everyday life and practices of mass consumption. This has determined how we have presented our material. Equal importance is given to graphic components as to narrative, and spatial analysis is prioritised. The conceptual unity of the material is manifested through a continuous dialogue with the creators of Zaporizhzhia Modernism – Yurii Biriukov, Tetiana Shchehlova, Svitlana Fomina, Serhii Prudkyi, Vadim Petrenko, Serhii Didenko, and Yevhen Holoshchapov – whose main works are presented in a separate section towards the end of the book. Original materials handed over by the architects were the primary source for our study and contributed to a better understanding of the circumstances and course of formation of Zaporizhzhia's modern urban space.

The publication of this book would not have been possible without the support of Philipp Meuser, Inna Stashchuk, Serhii Bilov, Valerii Hushcha, Oleh Burbovskyi, Nataliia Svitla, Dmytro Smolienko, Maksym Vokhin, Denis Novikov, Oleksandr Tedieiev, Yurii Kniazkov, Olena Velychko, Olha Volkova, Petro Boiko, Serhii Bilivnenko and the friendly staff at the Zaporizhzhia Museum of Architecture.

Pavlo Kravchuk,
Mykhailo Mordovskoi

A new morphology of the urban environment

The rapid urbanisation of the 1950s –1980s and the technological transition that took place at the end of the 1950s in the architectural and construction industry led to a fundamental change in the organisation of Zaporizhzhia's urban environment. Compact block development, visually defined in terms of clearly perceived geometric forms, ceased to meet the needs of society, in which the norm began to shift from observation of well-being to consumption of well-being. Spatially, this normative shift was shaped by the need to assimilate large undeveloped suburban areas intended for the creation of an infrastructure suitable for mass egalitarian unified consumption – unconstrained by the compositional rules of classical form-making. Instead of visual and compositional completeness, the main principle guiding the formation of residential, social, and cultural elements into so-called 'micro-districts' was now practical ease of access to services enterprises, calculated in terms of circles of 'pedestrian accessibility'. Planning of new territories was focused on public centres

A complex (large block) on the corner of Trade Union Square and Independent Ukraine Street, first half of the 1960s

Residential building on Bocharov Street, micro-district No. 1 in Shevchenkivskyi residential area, 1970

combining residential infrastructure with centres of labour and institutions and enterprises of city-wide importance. Mass public transport, in effect, produces dynamic series of images that form a coherent picture of the city – a picture that is capable of replacing the traditional urban laboratory of strolling. Dependent on the dynamics of urbanisation, the replication of new micro-districts, including their dense system of interconnections, is based on repeated reproduction of the impersonal properties of an urban space that is capable of accommodating normative numbers of people. An alternative to this approach that emerged in the first half of the 1960s was the concept of the 'New Settlement Element' (NSE), which focused on quantitative and qualitative constraints in order to ensure a positive course of socio-cultural processes during urbanisation. The authors of this concept proposed establishing limiting parameters for the 'social-spatial cell of the new society' (a town of up to 100,000), to move away from

THE
IN
FIN
ITY

of the micro-district model and provide a more individual solution for the urban environment. However, the main ideas of the NSE proved unable, in terms of both economics and technology and construction, to withstand competition from more flexible micro-district planning.

Development scheme for micro-district No. 100–101, Heorhii Vehman, 1958

Late 1950 to early 1960s. Returning to the experience of interwar Modernism

Micro-district No. 100–101, first half of the 1960s

Heorhii Vehman devised the development project for micro-district No. 100–101.
Vehman was a member of the editorial board of Sovremennaya arkhitektura *(SA), the journal of the Association of Modern Architects, 1926–1930.*

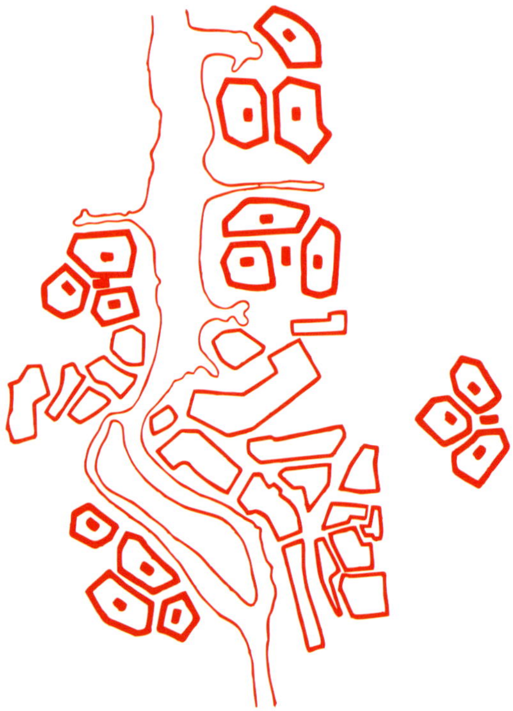

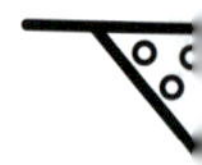

Territorial development of the city under the general plan of 1965

Scheme of the architectural and planning structure of the city under the general plan of 1965

The first half of the 1960s. Identification of areas for integrated development

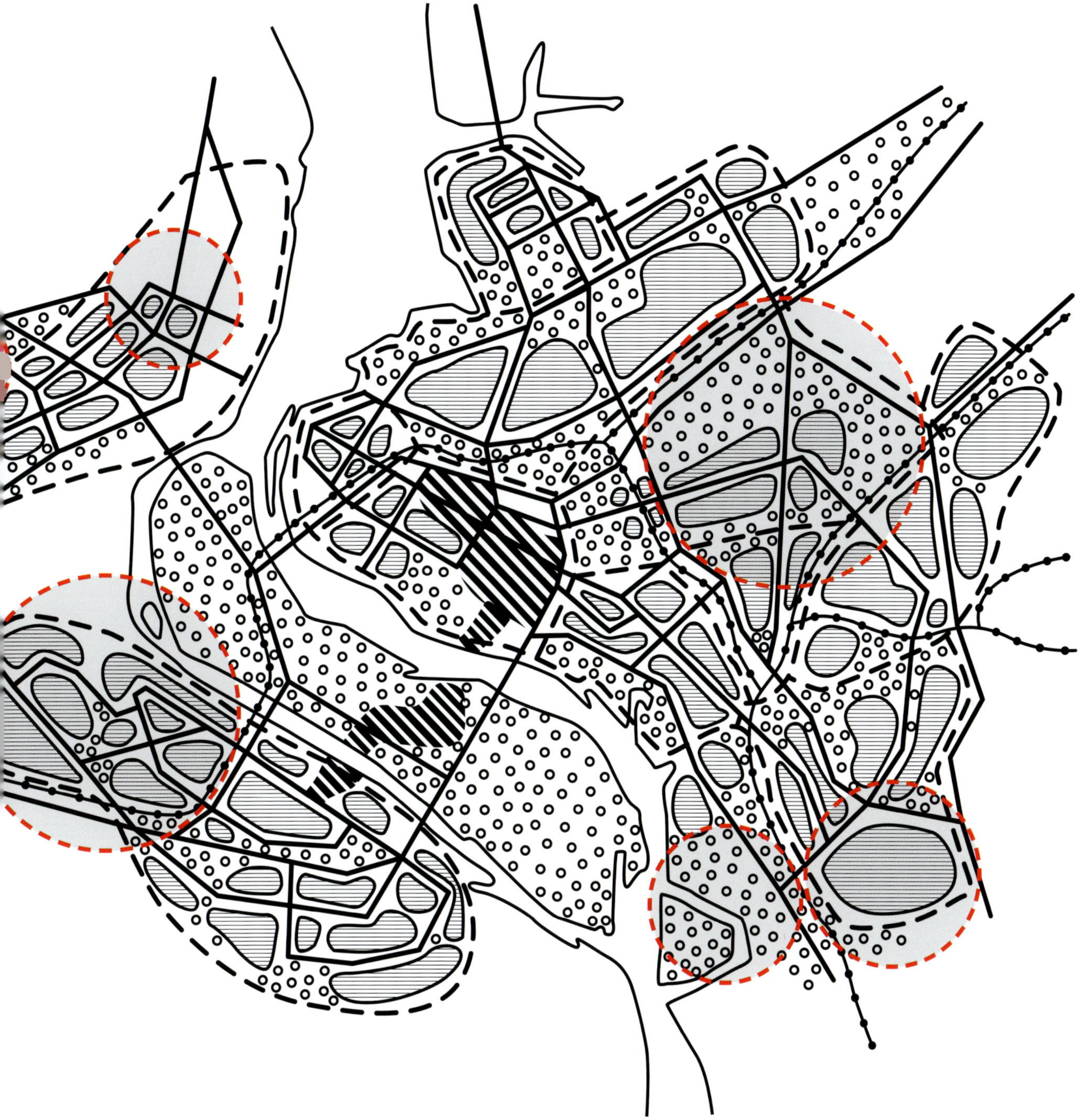

1

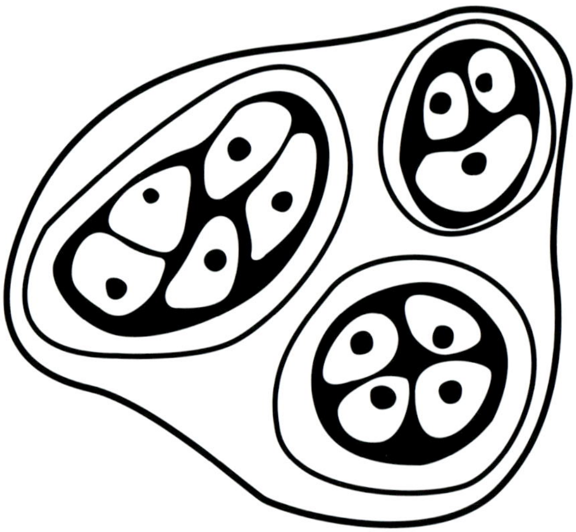

1. Cellular structure of a living organism: nucleus and protoplasm
2. Scheme showing urban-planning formations. A: city centre; B: residential area; C: micro-district; D: basic residential group.
Author of the comparison: Heorhii Hradov, 1968

2

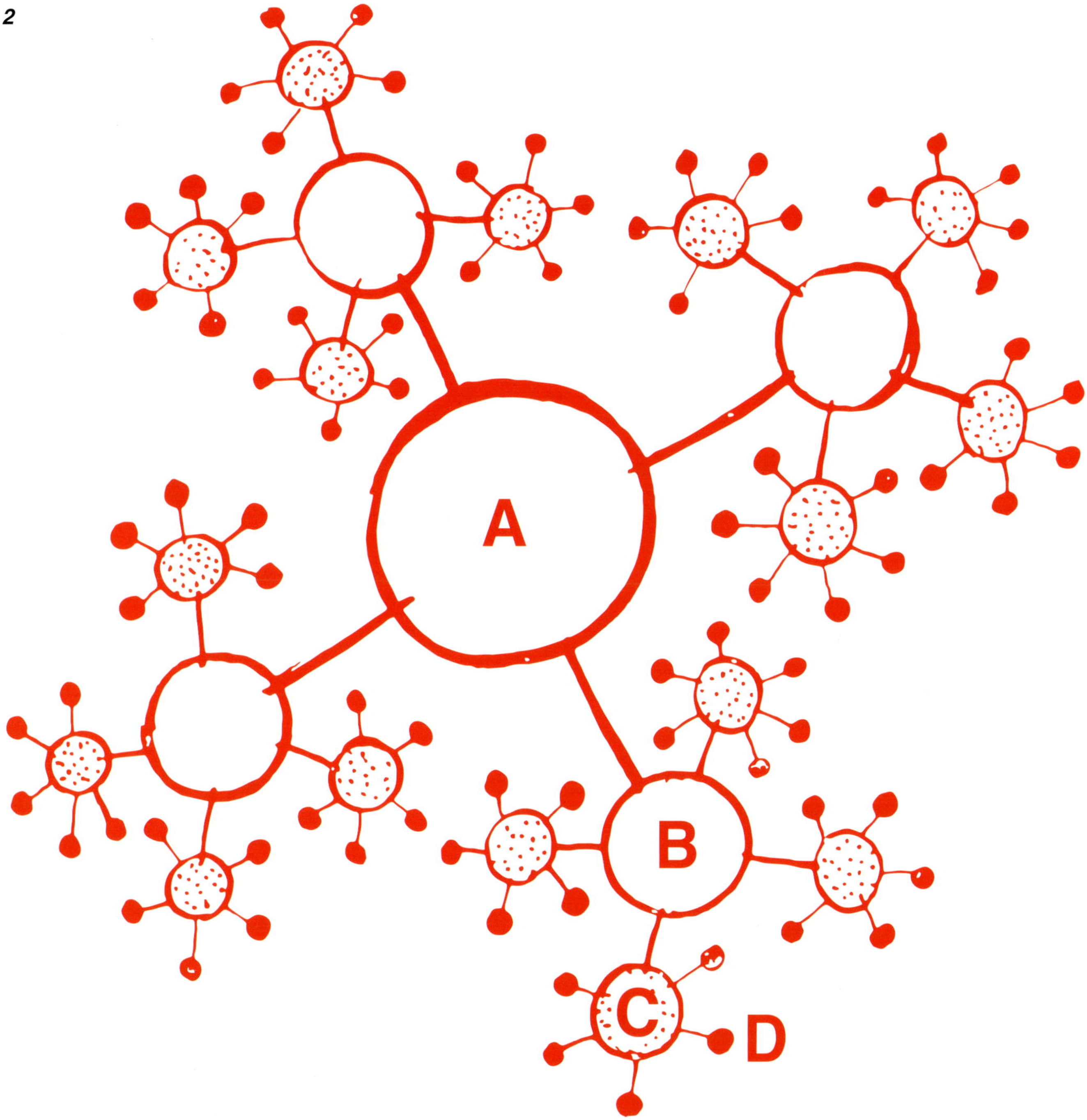

A — public complex of city-wide importance; 1 — administrative and cultural centre; 2 — shopping centre; 3 — sports centre; 4 — medical centre; 5 — specialised hospitals; 6 — city park; 7 — research and educational complex; 8 — economic and communal complex; 9 — unified railway station

B — public complex of the city district; cooperative district administrative building (including communication facilities and credit institutions); movie and concert hall, specialised club, shopping centre, CSE, secondary technical educational institution, district hospital with polyclinic, stadium

C — community centre of the residential area

D — public centre of the industrial district

E — industrial enterprise

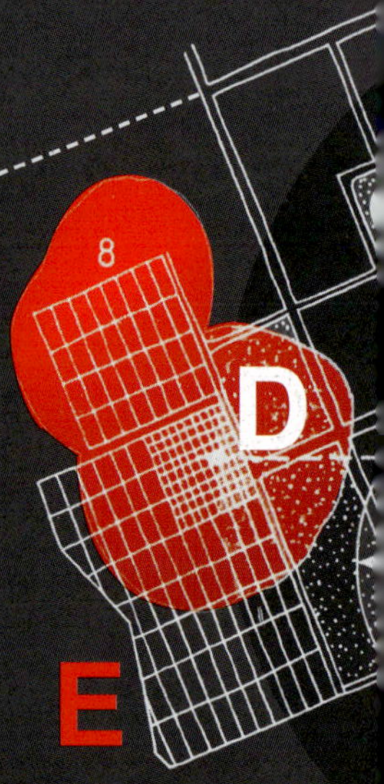

Author of the scheme: Heorhii Hradov, 1968.

Basic scheme of service and production networks for the new urban space

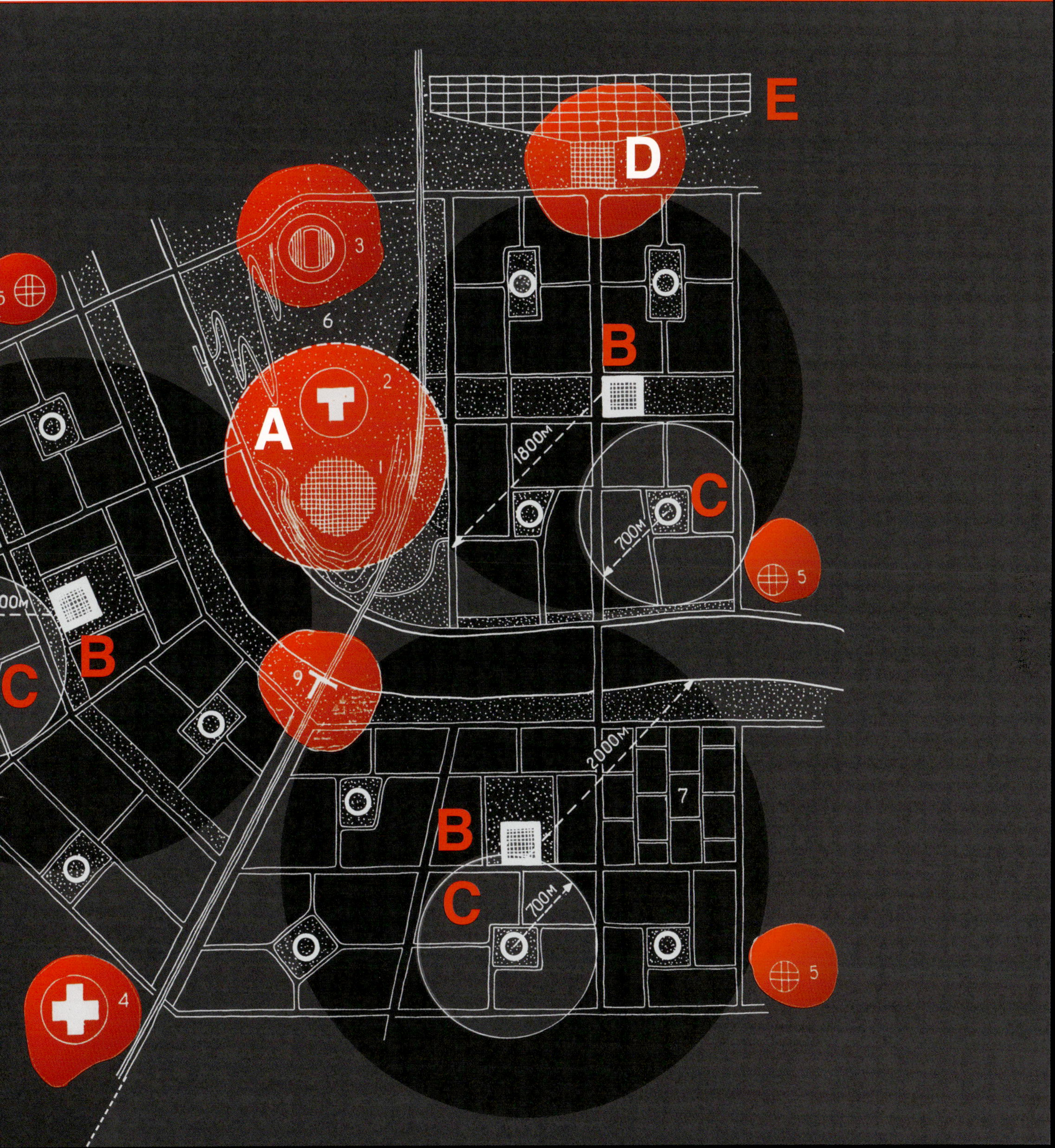

1960s. Enlargement of the scale of urban-planning form

Residential area on Kosmichne Highway, Zaporizhzhia branch of Ukrmiskbudproject, first half of the 1960s

Запорожье шевченковский р-н, микрорайон №1

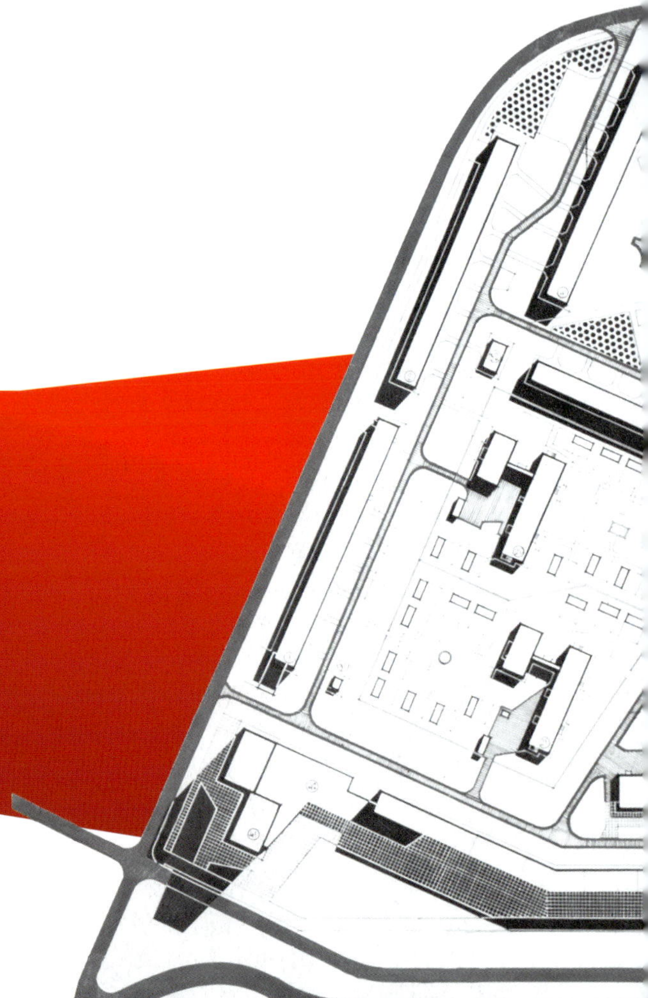

Development scheme for micro-district No. 1 in Shevchenkivskyi residential area, Zaporizhzhia branch of Ukrmiskbudproject, 1966

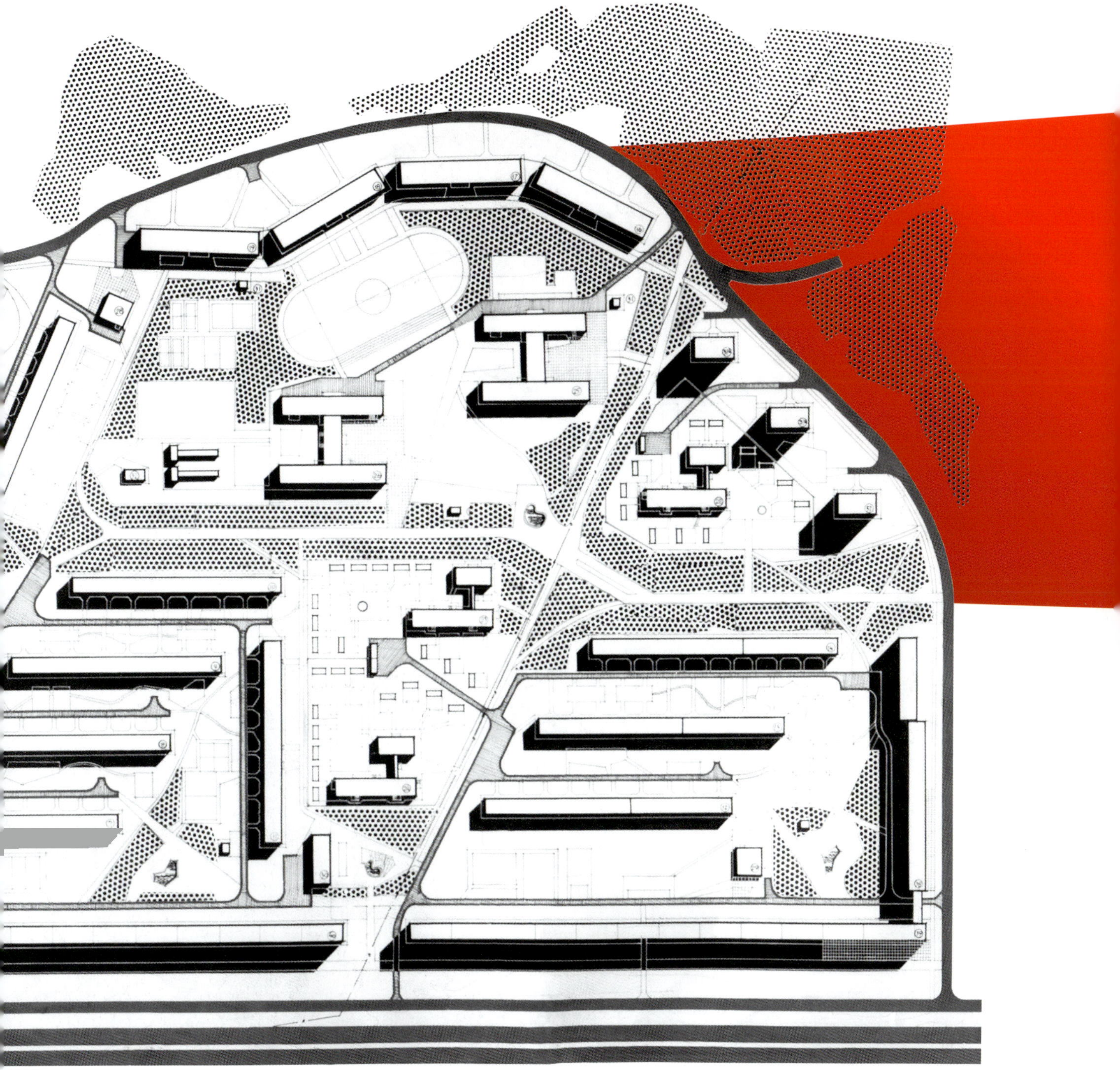

'The development of the city of Zaporizhzhia is being carried out in accordance with the general plan approved by the Council of Ministers of the Ukrainian SSR on 13 May 1966. To date, the construction of the entire central part of the city has been completed, and housing construction is being carried out mainly on the outskirts of the city – on Kosmichne Highway, in the Shevchenkivskyi district, and on the right bank. Preparations are underway for the start of construction in a new large area on the right bank (Dniprobud-II). In the city's central area selective construction of public buildings and individual residential buildings is being carried out.'

From an official report sent by V. Morhulets, the head of the regional department for construction and architecture, to the construction department of the regional committee of the Communist Party of Ukraine (13 March 1969)

Development scheme for micro-district No. 2 in Shevchenkivskyi residential area, Zaporizhzhia branch of Ukrmiskbudproject, 1967

Draft proposal for the formation of a public and commercial centre for micro-districts Nos. 1–2 in the Shevchenkivskyi residential area, Yurii Biriukov

1960s. Enlargement of the scale of urban-planning form

NSE

Spatial localisation of the system of forms of communication under communism determines the functional structure of the settlement. Each type of building is interpreted as an element of this single, all-pervading structure.

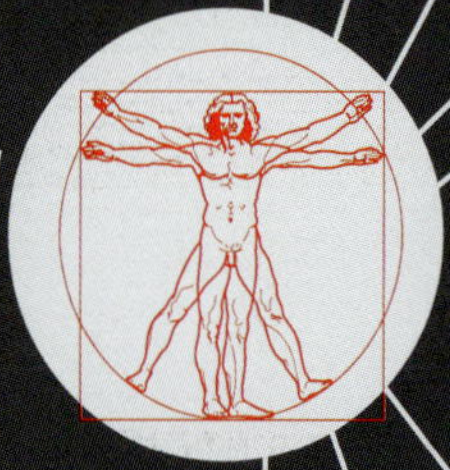

Childhood
/mother and newborn/

Blood-family communication
/family/

Communication between children
/children as a team/

Education
/educational team/

Manufacturing communication during the required working hours */creative team/*

Free communication
1/ work in free time
2/ on-job training
3/ communication based on interests
4/ social life
5/ solitude /free collectives/

Consumer communication

Intersex communication

Person in the system of forms of communication

Forms of communication and social units

NSE: the officially approved urban-planning alternative

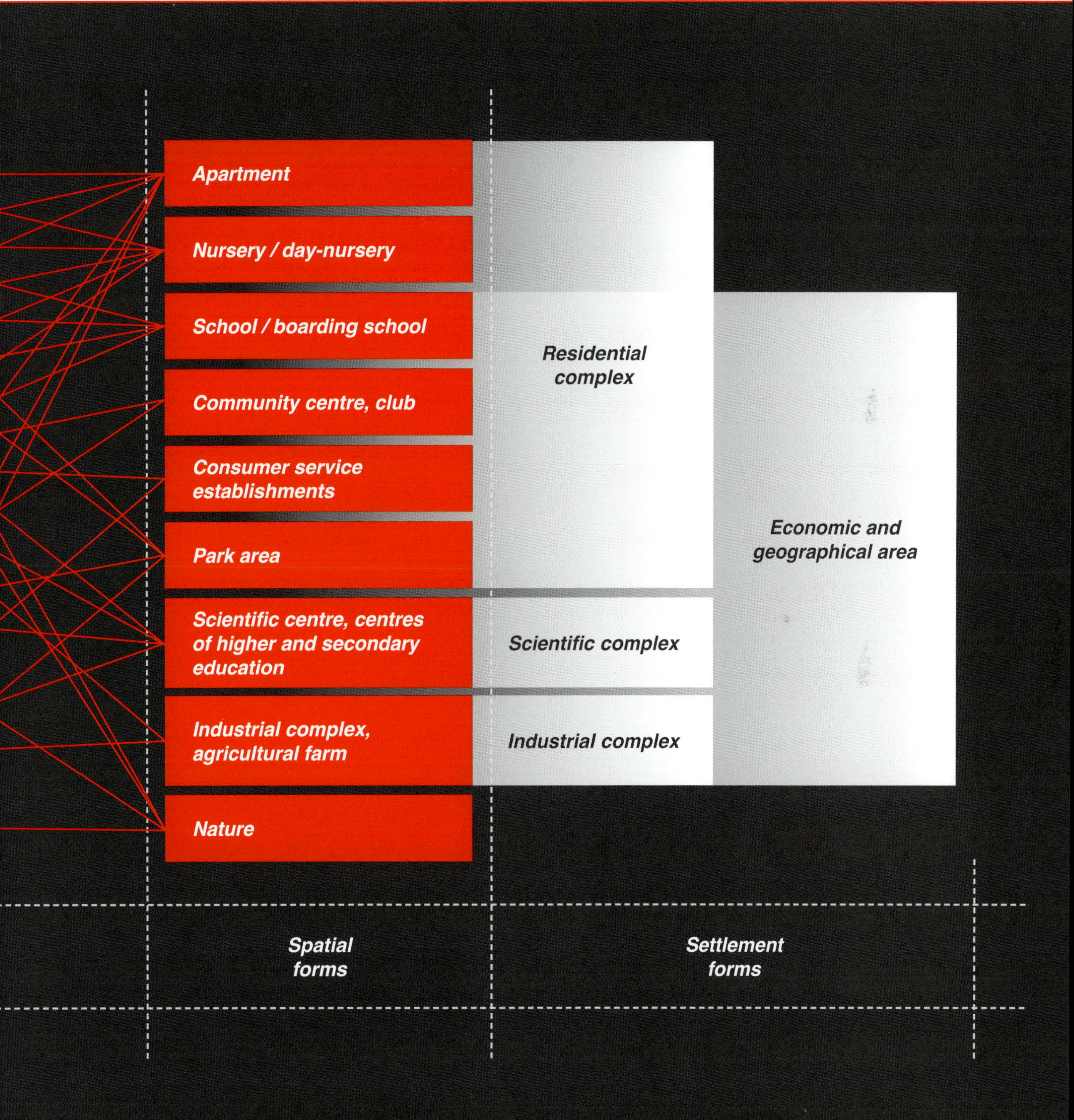

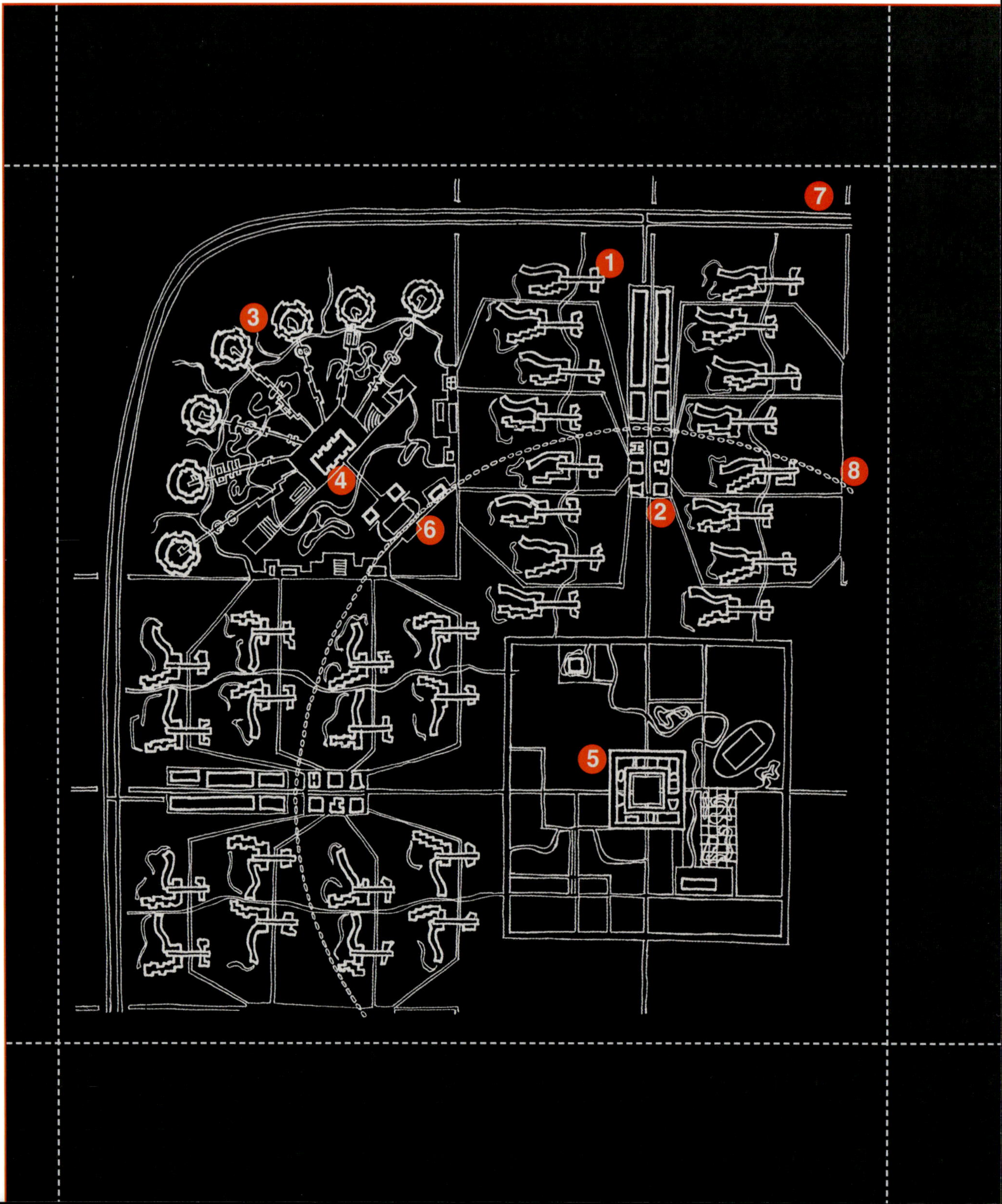
1
2
3
4
5
6
7
8

NSE: the officially approved urban-planning alternative

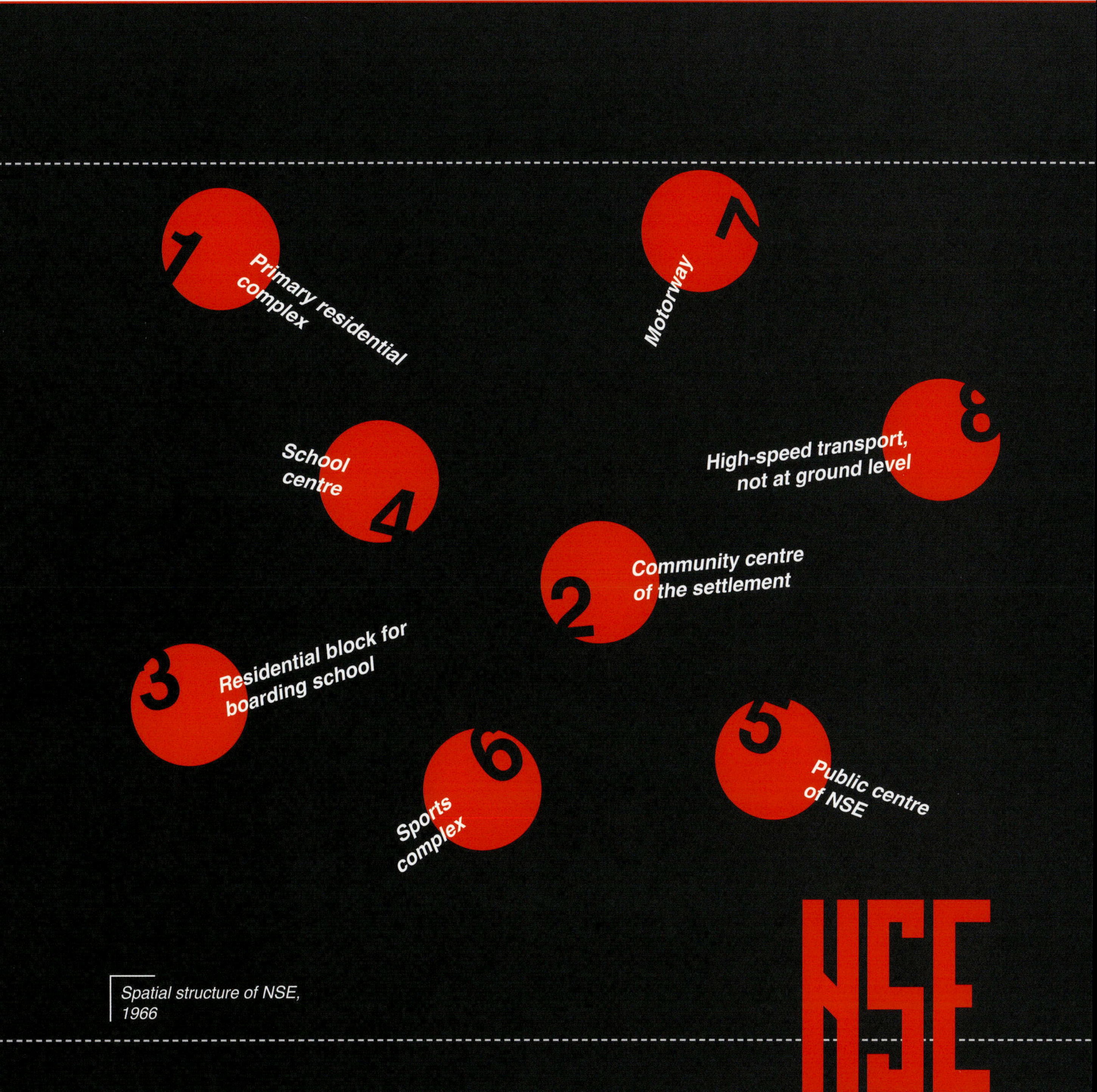

Spatial structure of NSE, 1966

Development of the Dniprobud-II residential area, seen against the background of micro-district No. 7 (Khortytskyi), 1970s

'Each residential area has a centre that brings together the main institutions regularly used by citizens. Each micro-district has its own centre with facilities for daily use. The development is composed in such a way as to reveal and emphasise the terrain, creating a picturesque panorama from the direction of Khortytsia Island and the left bank of the River Dnipro. Its design combines a regular rhythm of multi-storey buildings with free arrangement of individual groups of multi-storey buildings. The micro-district is built up with large groups of residential buildings that form semi-enclosed spaces. The rejection of micro-district gardens in favour of large groups and the increase in the number of storeys and in the length of the houses allow us to increase the scale of the development.'

From a speech by O. Rapoport, a representative of Dipromisto, on the compositional design of the Dniprobud-II residential area (1963)

Plan showing development of the Dniprobud-II (Khortytskyi) residential area, first half of the 1970s

Draft proposal for formation of a public and commercial centre for micro-district No. 3 (not implemented), Dniprobud-II residential area, Yurii Biriukov

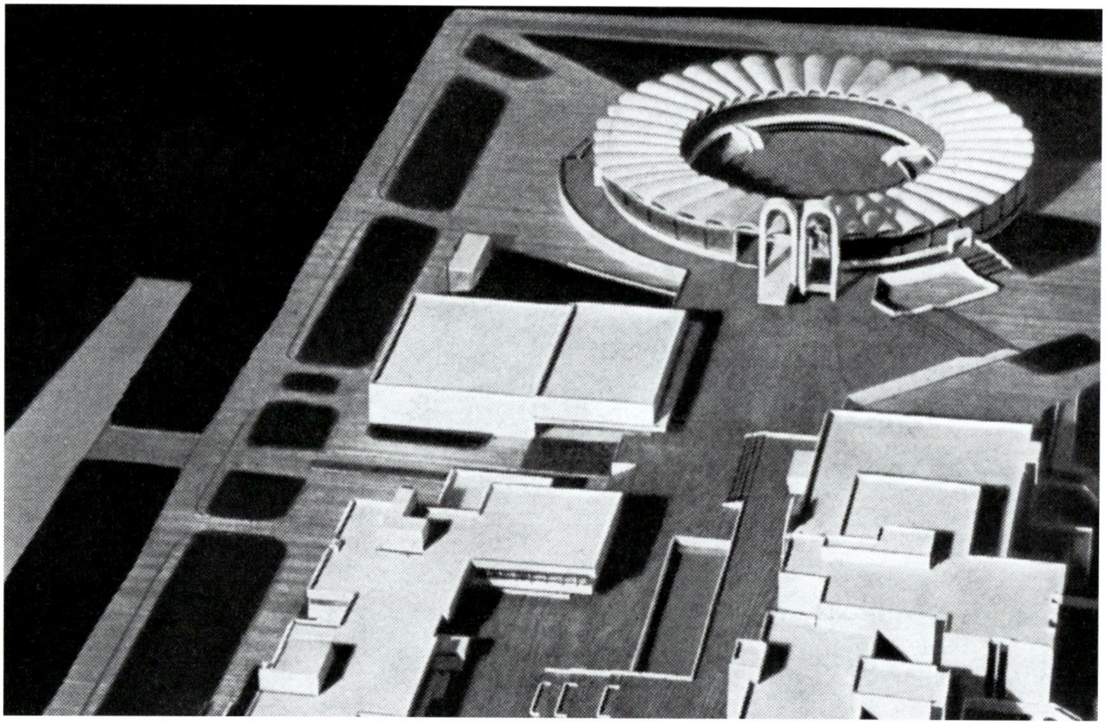

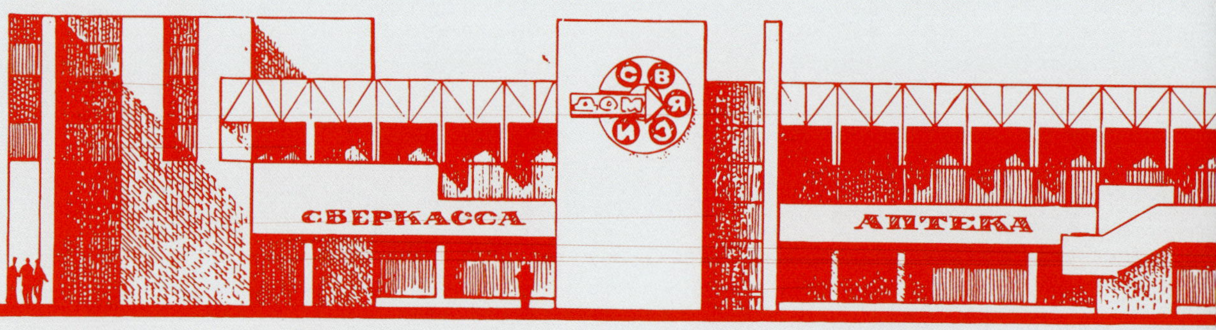

Public and shopping centre for the Dniprobud-II residential area, design proposal, first half of the 1970s. Central Scientific Research Institute for Standardised and Experimental Design of Trade and Service Buildings and Tourist Complexes. Architects: E. Bikson, V. Leonov, V. Timofieiev. Engineers: Yu. Lievitin, H. Ratnovskaia

К
книги

Micro-district No. 1 in the Osypenkivskyi residential area, layout, 1978

Borodinskyi residential area, layout, design institute "Zaporizhtsyvilproject", 1985.

Micro-district (Bombay) on Serhii Synenko Street, layout, Zaporizhtsyvilproject, second half of the 1980s

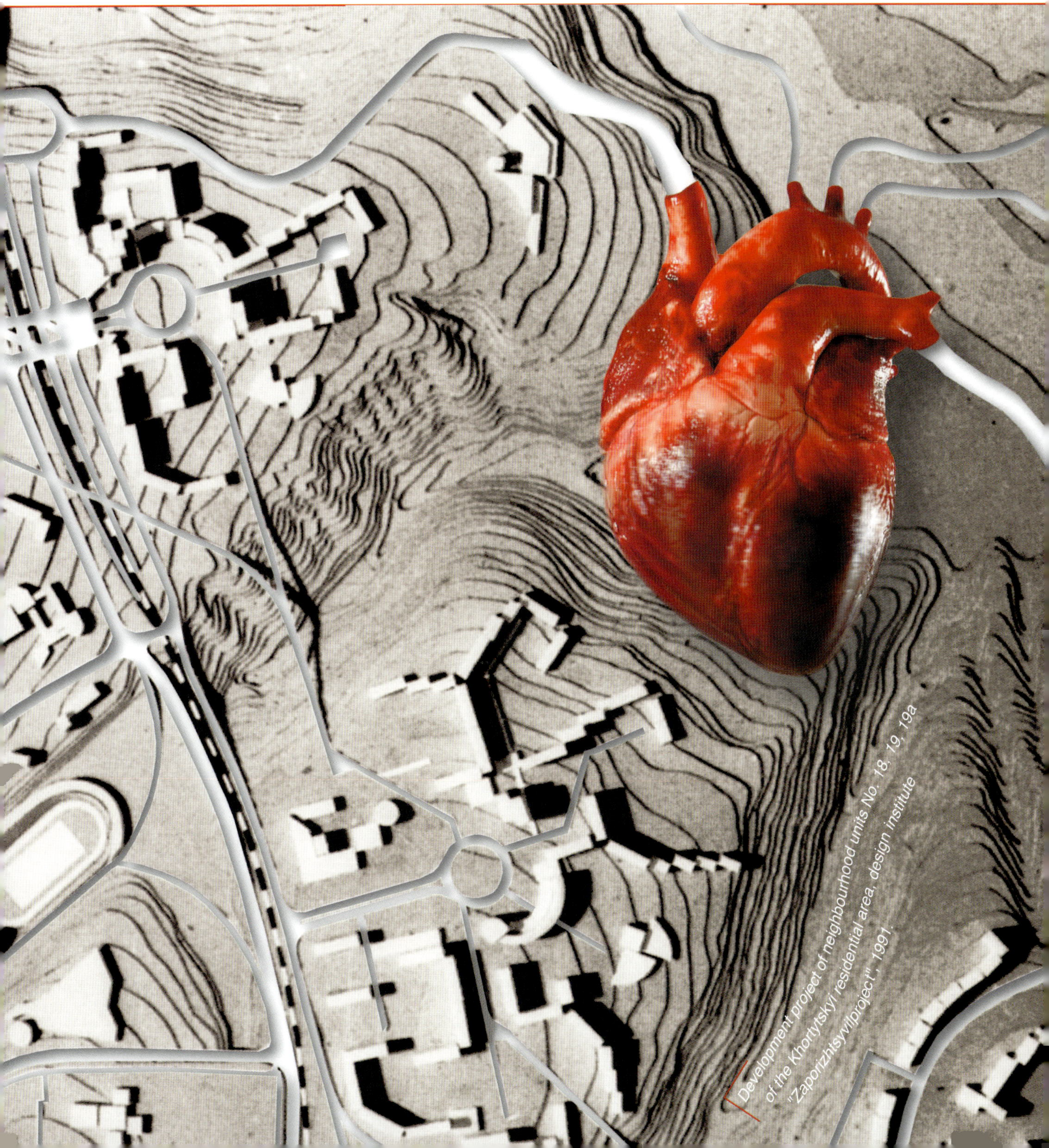

Development project of neighbourhood units No. 18, 19, 19a of the Khortytskyi residential area, design institute "Zaporizhtsyvilproject", 1991.

Development project for the territory of Voznesenivskyi Market, layout, Serhii Prudkyi (as member of creative team)

Progress in organisational culture and construction techniques

Industrialisation of production was the general leitmotif of the Soviet architectural and construction industry during the 1950s. Even the great Neoclassical ensembles in major cities such as Zaporizhzhia were built using contemporary industrial methods based on the use of standardised projects and building details. There was likewise an increase in the degree of mechanisation of production sites. The first tower crane appeared in Zaporizhzhia in 1945. However, the existing degree of mechanisation and industrialisation was not sufficient to enable mass rehousing of citizens in individual apartments. The resolution of the Central Committee of the CPSU and the Council of Ministers of the USSR 'On the Development of Housing Construction in the USSR' (1957) announced a move towards qualitatively new organisational and technical frontiers in housing production. 'Construction of large residential areas' using panel and block prefabricated structures was introduced. To a large extent, the Soviet Union adopted the experience of other European countries – above all, France, which had achieved notable success in construction of prefabricated panel buildings.

For the domestic architectural and construction industry, the technological transition outlined by the state leadership meant more stringent requirements for engineering preparation and equipment of the territories of residential areas, which in effect became autonomous micro-districts. The new complex issues led not only to the reorganisation of the entire industry and the formation of large territorial trusts and production associations (Zaporizhbuddetal, Zaporizhtsyvilbud) and customer services (the city's Capital Construction Department), but also to a change in the psychology of production itself. Multi-storey buildings were now seen as volumetric elements of the neighbourhood development in general. In some cases the engineering and geological preparations for a residential unit with local experimental plots took more effort and time than the construction of entire groups of 'volumetric elements'. Examples are micro-districts in the

Khortytskyi and Pivdennyi residential areas. The introduction of prefabricated house-construction technologies was no less a challenge than the engineering preparation of the territories. Improvement of these technologies most commonly occurred post factum: complaints from tenants and building managers led to special commissions being set up to identify deficiencies in both standardised construction parts and the course of construction and installation work. The elimination of recorded organisational and technical failures became its own genre of production bureaucracy. In general, in 1960–1980 the organisational culture of mass housing construction was characterised by the introduction of network planning to ensure a stable rhythm of work and avoid 'storm surges'. Appropriate instruction manuals and instruction booklets for Zaporizhzhia enterprises and services were prepared for the first time by the Dnipropetrovsk branch of the Scientific and Research Institute of Construction Production.

Large-panel housing-construction plant

1 — pumpcrete pipe
2 — self-propelled bunker with trailer
3 — production line for exterior wall panels
4 — pit chambers
5 — exterior-wall-panel finishing conveyor
6 — moulds for specialised products
7 — device for forming voids in products
8 — pit chambers
9 — cassettes for forming panels
10 — trolley for removal of finished products

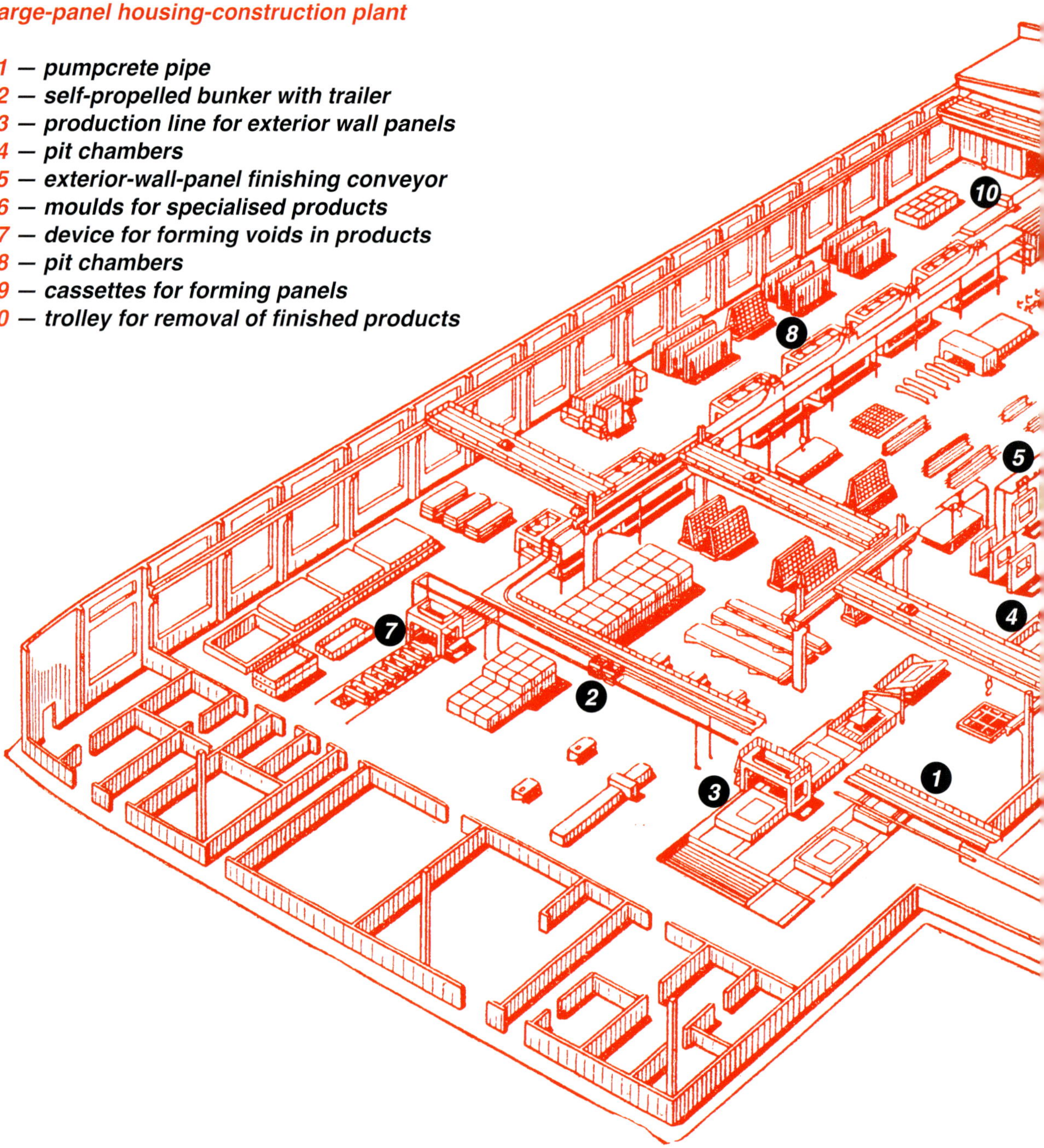

Late 1950s. The transition to prefabricated housing technologies

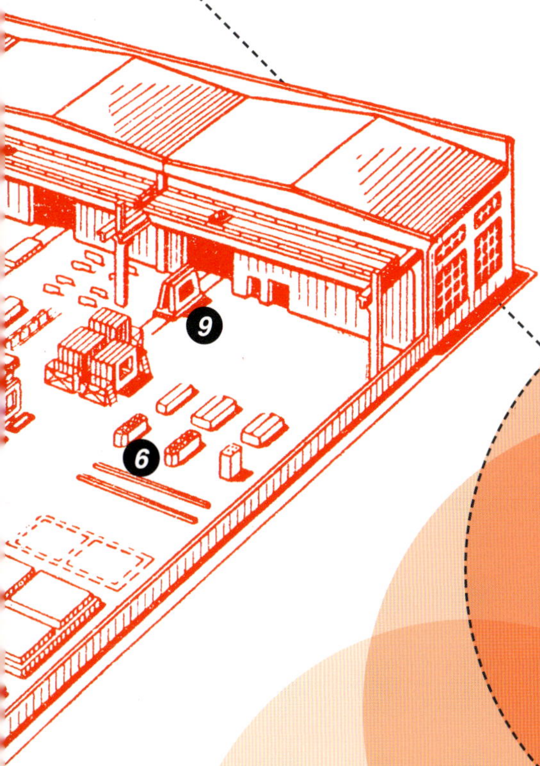

Ivan Shchehlov, organiser of large-panel housing construction:
1959–1964: head of Zaporizhbuddetal
1964–1973: head of Zaporizhzhia Capital Construction Department

Late 1950s to mid-1960s. Large-panel construction in inner-city areas

Complex development of micro-district No. 100–101 in the vicinity of Viacheslav Zaitsev Street, 1959. Use of standardised designs from series 1-437, 1-438, 1-444-3, 1-445-3, 1-464п, and 1-480п

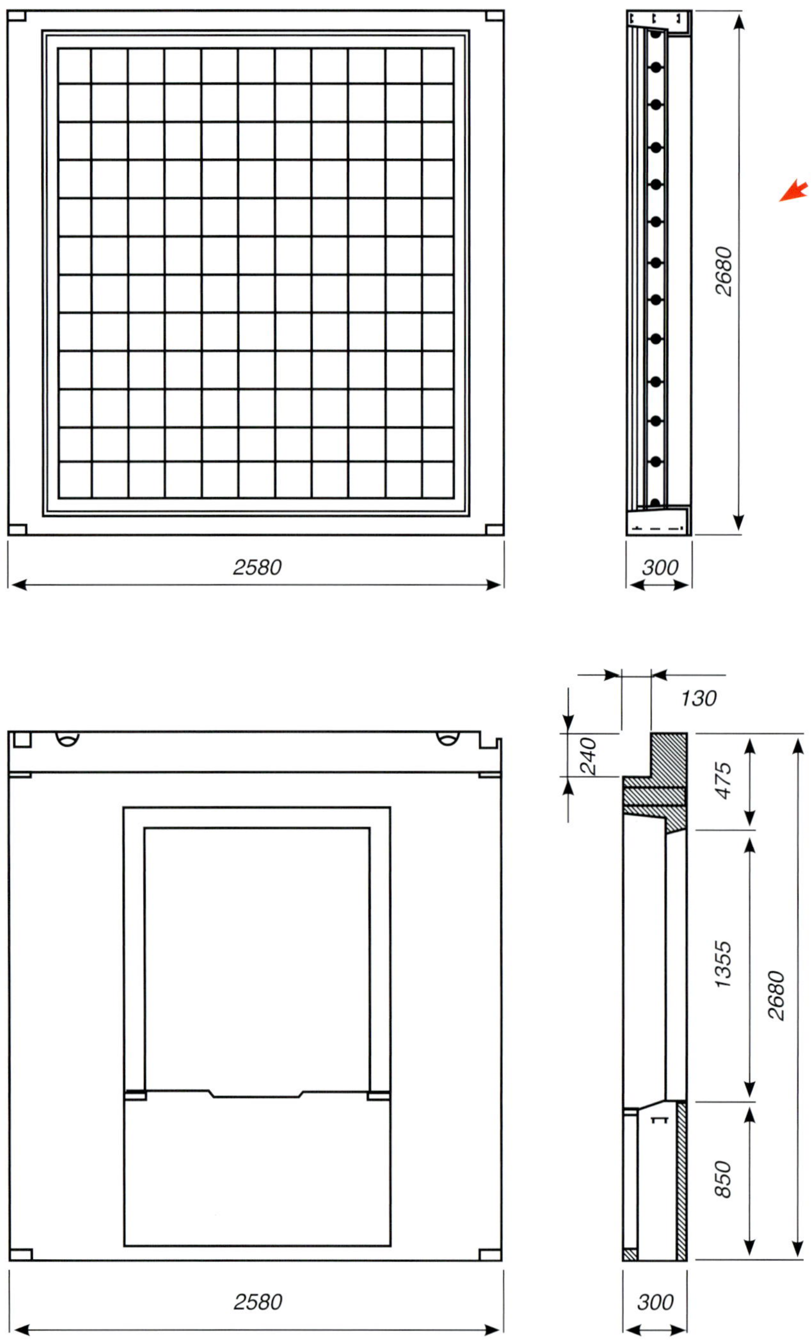

Diagram showing construction and assembly of a large-panel residential building from Series 1-480

Late 1950s to mid-1960s. Large-panel construction in inner-city areas

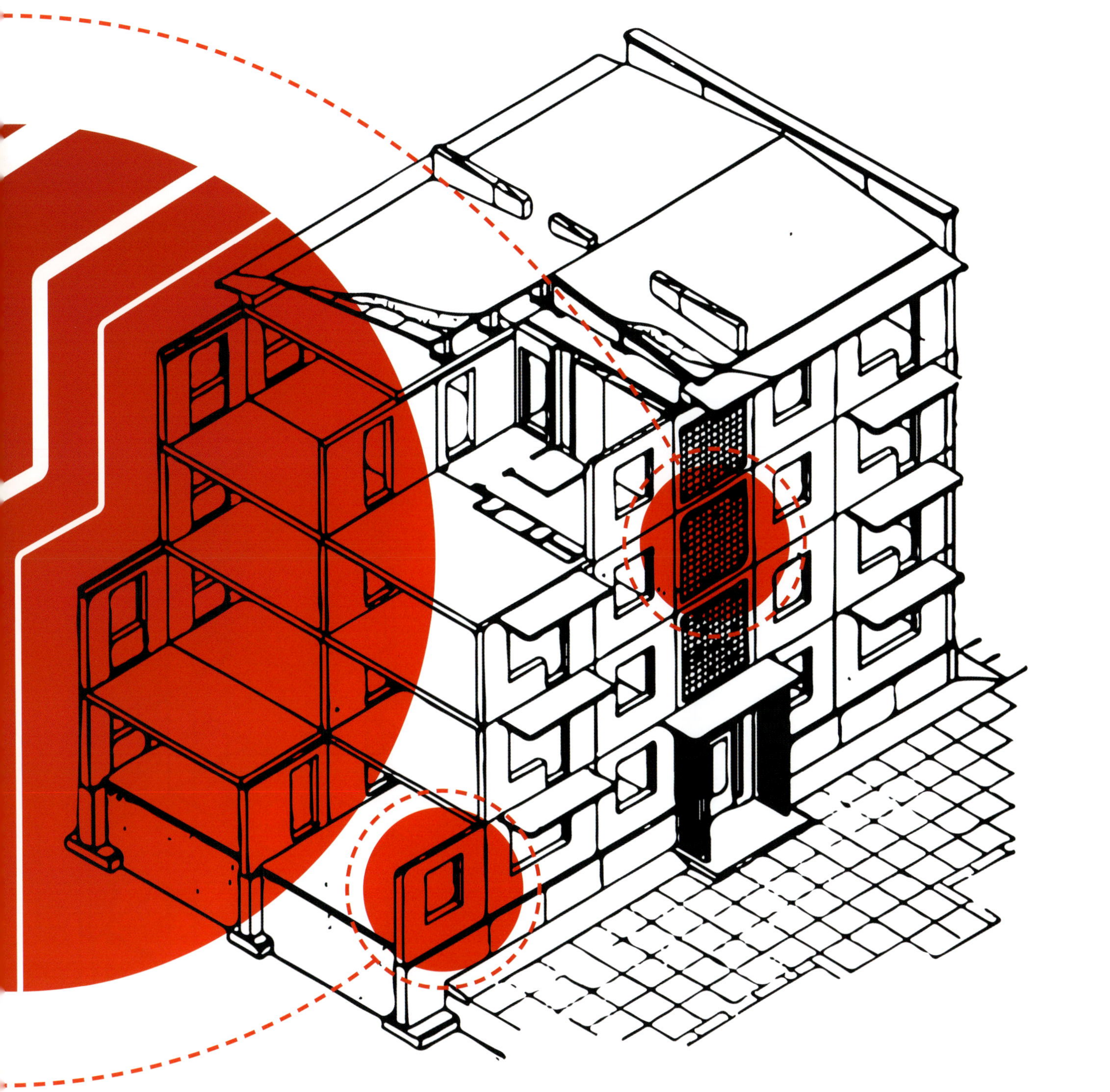

Large-block construction in the Central District (Voznesenka), 1959

Panel construction in the Central District (Voznesenka), 1959

Micro-district No. 3 in the Dniprobud-II residential area, 1979. Construction of a complex of residential buildings

Late 1960s to 1970s. Development of new areas with houses from Series 480A

A part of the façade decoration and the design of the building entrance

Driveway in the central part of the house. The blind side walls are decorated with ornaments of coloured glazed ceramic tiles of the 'kabanchyk' type.

Photo: Igor Lavrov, 2020

'What kind of residential buildings will there be? The existing house-building factory [on the left bank] will provide 210,000 square metres a year. It produces Series 480 houses. The equipment of the mill will be improved. Its output will account for 51 per cent of prefabricated housing construction. Then Series 96. This will be introduced at the new factory [on the right bank], which will produce its first output in 1978, including 17 per cent of large-block houses and 15 per cent of brick houses. The total percentage of prefabrication in house building will be 85%.'

From a speech by Sergiy Vasylevskyi, chief architect of Zaporizhzhia, at the scientific and technical council of the State Construction Committee of the Ukrainian SSR, 9 June 1976

Residential development with houses from Series 96. Micro-district No. 17 in the Khortytskyi residential area

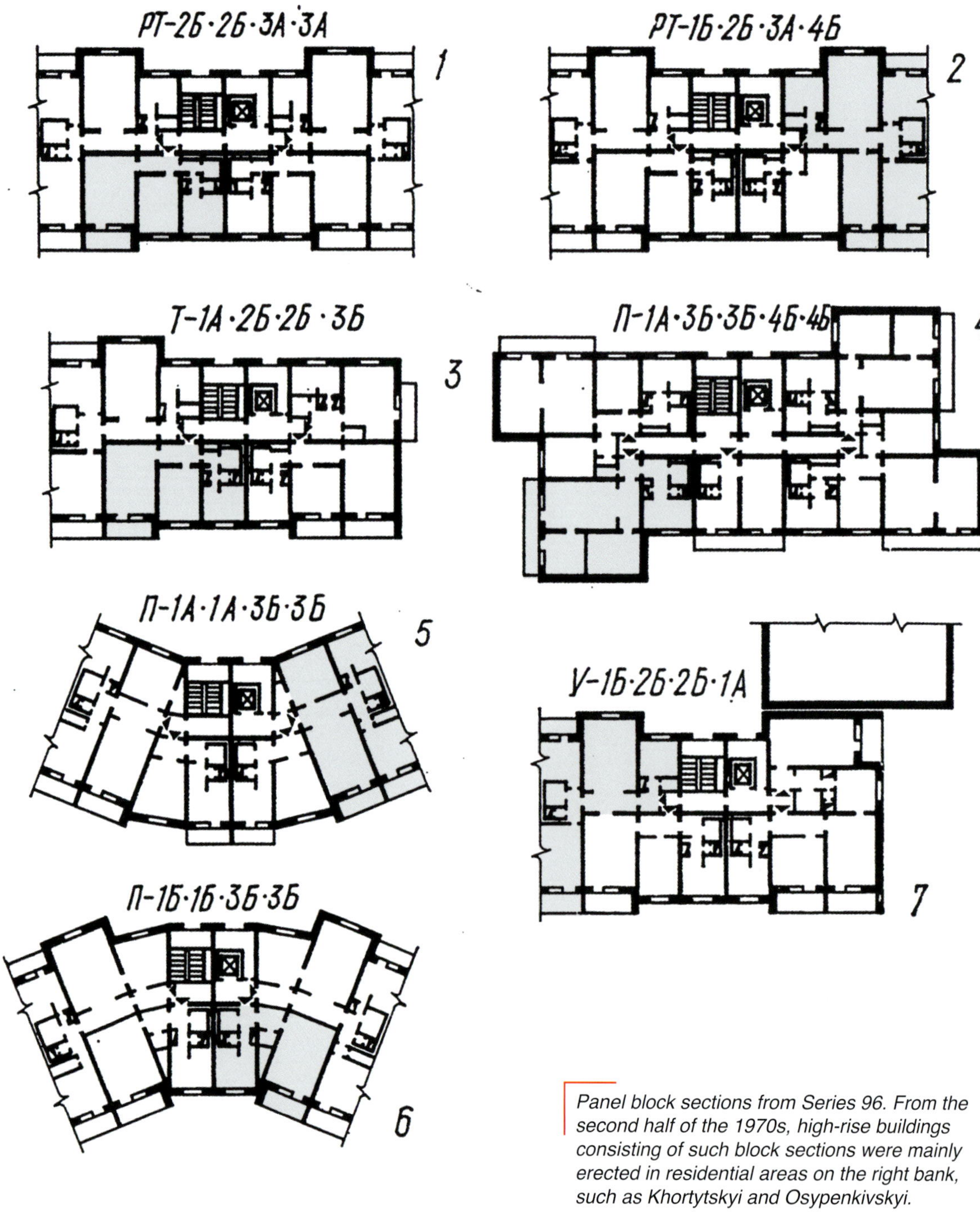

Panel block sections from Series 96. From the second half of the 1970s, high-rise buildings consisting of such block sections were mainly erected in residential areas on the right bank, such as Khortytskyi and Osypenkivskyi.

Late 1970s to 1980s. Mass construction of houses from Series 96

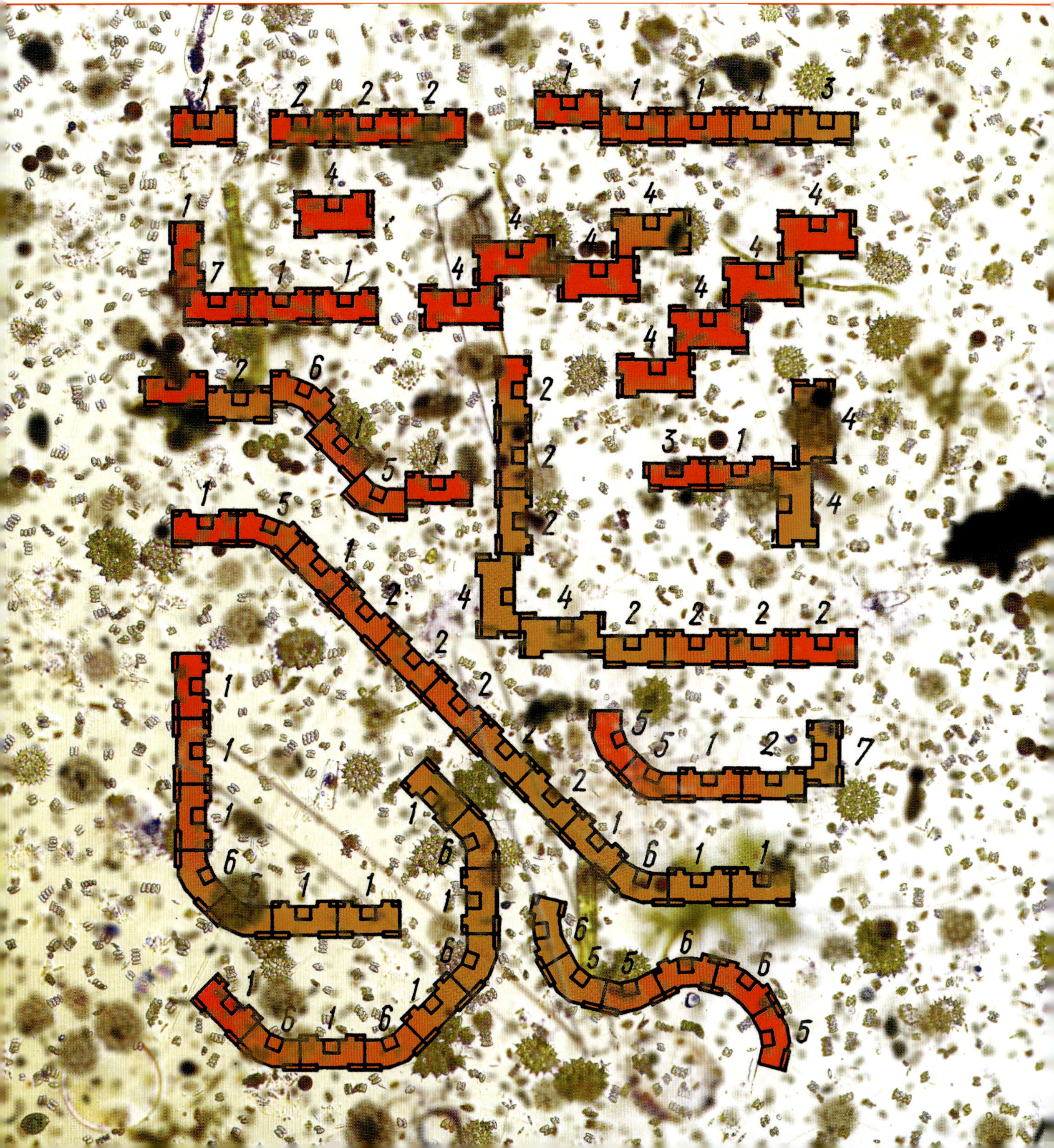

'During the construction of micro-districts "on Baburka" [the Khortytskyi residential area], the main problem was the soil conditions — the great thickness of the collapsible soils. Research institutes at USSR level were involved in eliminating subsidence in soils used for the construction of houses. In particular, this territory was the experimental site of the Gersevanov Research Institute of Bases and Underground Structures, Moscow. In addition, the State Research Institute of Building Constructions (Zaporizhzhia branch) dealt with the problem of liquidation of collapsible soils. Its findings were incorporated in regulatory documents that applied throughout the USSR. In particular, for micro-districts 15, 16, 17, and 18, the most effective elimination method – hydraulic explosion – was chosen. As a result, the structure of the soil changed and the subsidence properties were eliminated, which made it possible to quickly and reliably build nine-storey houses. The Pivdennyi residential area was also designed on a difficult terrain – water-logged soil. The engineering preparation of this territory involved sand alluvium, which, by the way, is the most reliable foundation on which to construct buildings. The main problem in engineering preparation was to determine the depth of the layer of sand that needed to be added. The following factors were taken into account: rising groundwater and flood water; wave height in the event

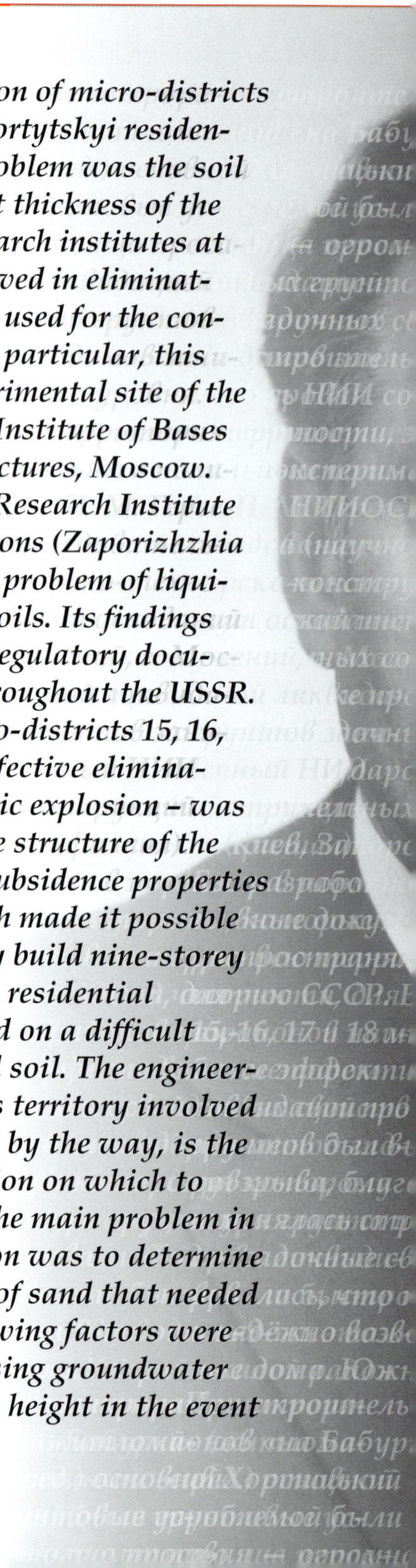

Mykola Petrenko, organiser of mass housing construction, chief engineer and deputy director of Zaporizhtsyvilbud production association in 1972–1987

of failure of the Dnipro Hydroelectric Dam. Specialised water-management institutions were involved in the decision-making, as well as the Civil Defence Headquarters. The coordinator of these works was V. Stefanchuk, the principal architect for this project at Zaporizhtsyvilproject Institute. The depth of the reclamation layer was taken as five metres on average, and this decision was reviewed and approved by the State Construction Committee of the Ukrainian SSR. In other areas of the city the soils were characterised by "moderate" subsidence, and there were no special requirements when planning micro-districts.'

From answers given by Vadim Petrenko, chief architect at Zaporizhtsyvilproject, to the questionnaire developed as part of the 'Zaporizhzhia. Micro-districts' urban-history project (2021)

'Sixty hectares of territory are to be developed by the method of alluvial land reclamation. After looking at similar territories in Donetsk and Kyiv and after appropriate consultations, we decided on the best option. The plan is to inwash soil to depths of between 1.5 and 7 metres and equip the territory with a system of drainage canals.' 'The residential area will be covered with 9-12-16-storey houses based on Series 96 and houses built to one-off projects on the most important urban-planning sites – at the entrance to the residential area, on the embankment, and in the vicinity of the shopping centre.'

From a speech by Yurii Biriukov, director of Zaporizhtsyvilproject Design Institute, at the scientific and technical council of the State Construction Committee of the Ukrainian SSR, 4 November 1981

Land set aside for future development of the Pivdennyi residential area, 1970s

The first phase of development of the Pivdennyi residential area, mid-1980s

1980s. Land reclamation

Construction of an experimental 16-storey residential building of monolithic construction using volumetric mobile formwork, 1985. This project was developed by Kyiv Zonal Scientific Research Institute for Standardised and Experimental Design of Residential and Public Buildings, with reference to Zaporizhtsyvilproject Design Institute (principal project architect: Oleksandr Yehorov).

Total Modernism

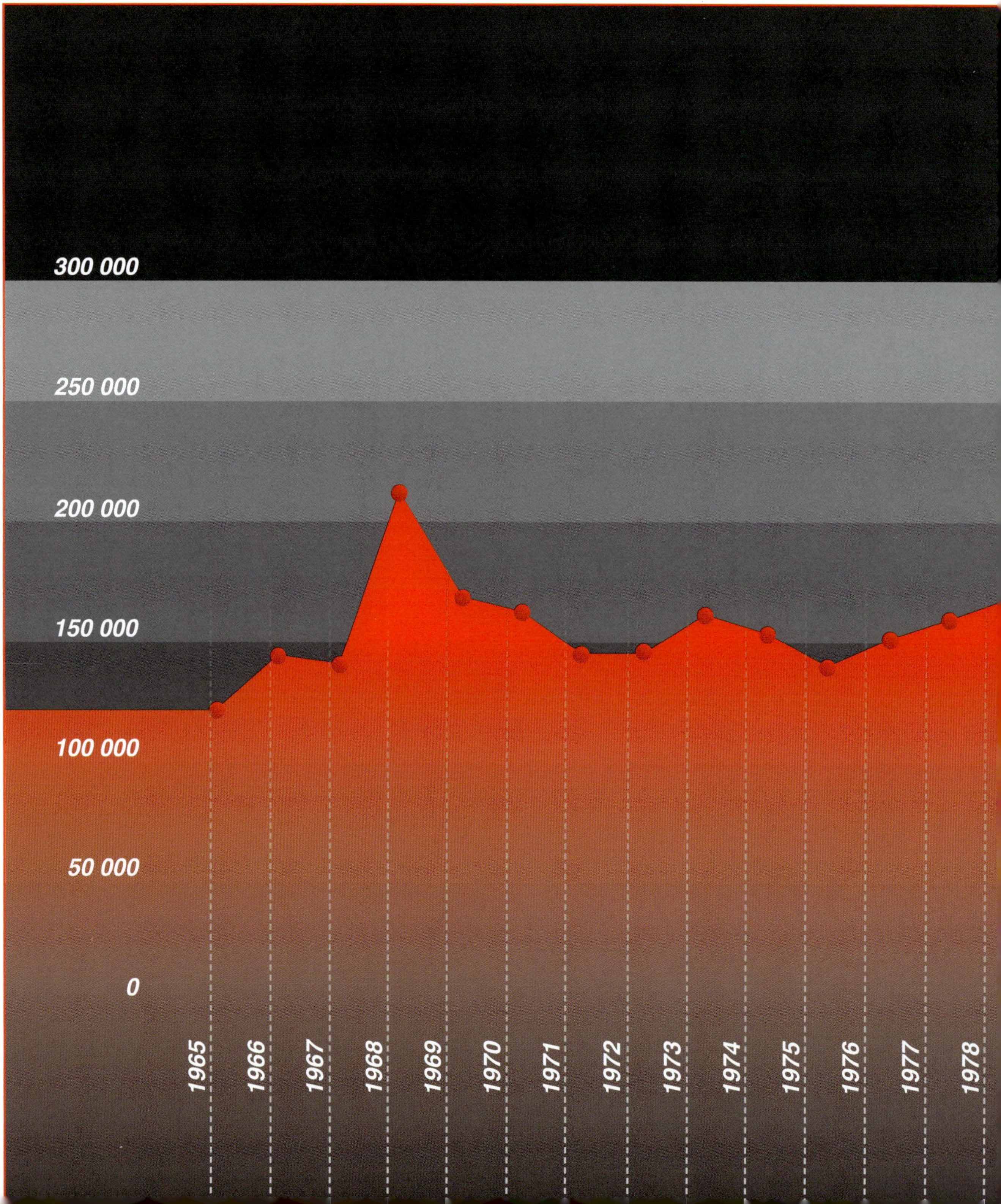

Volumes of residential construction by the Capital Construction Department in 1965– 1996 (in square metres), according to data supplied by Nastroi LLC

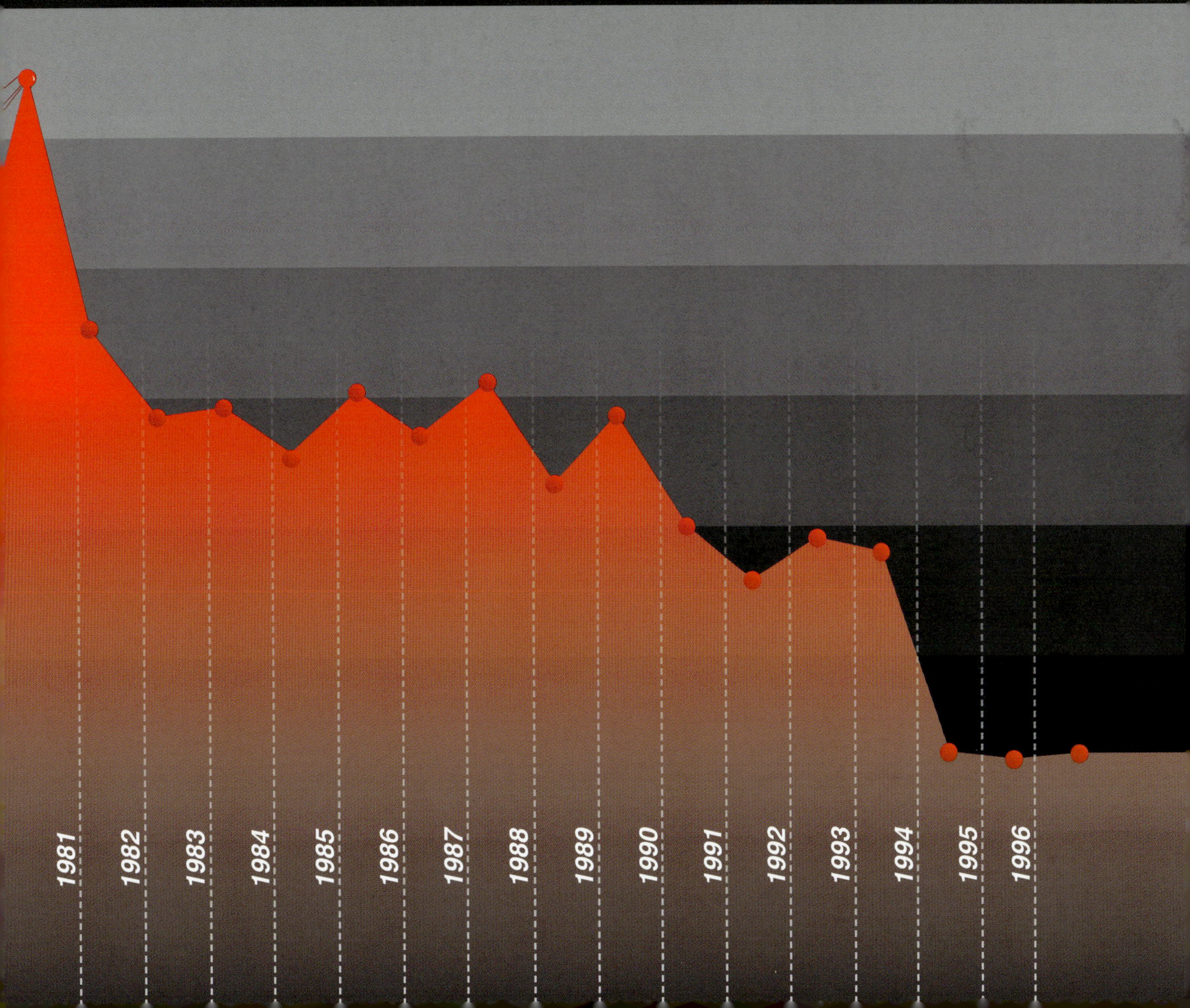

Total Modernism

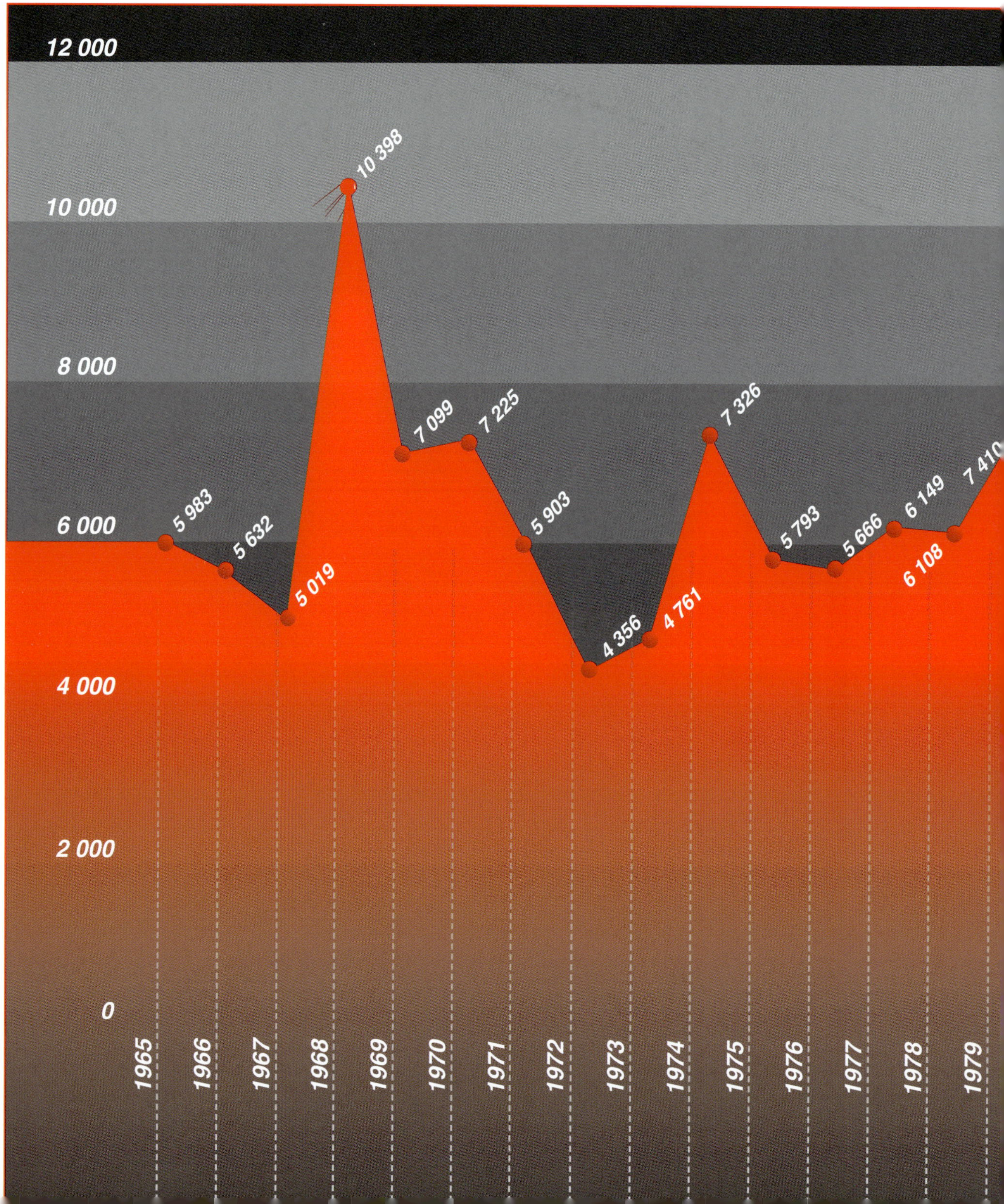

1960s – 1990s. General dynamics of residential construction

Number of individual apartments in residential buildings built by the Capital Construction Department in 1965– 1996, according to data supplied by Nastroi LLC

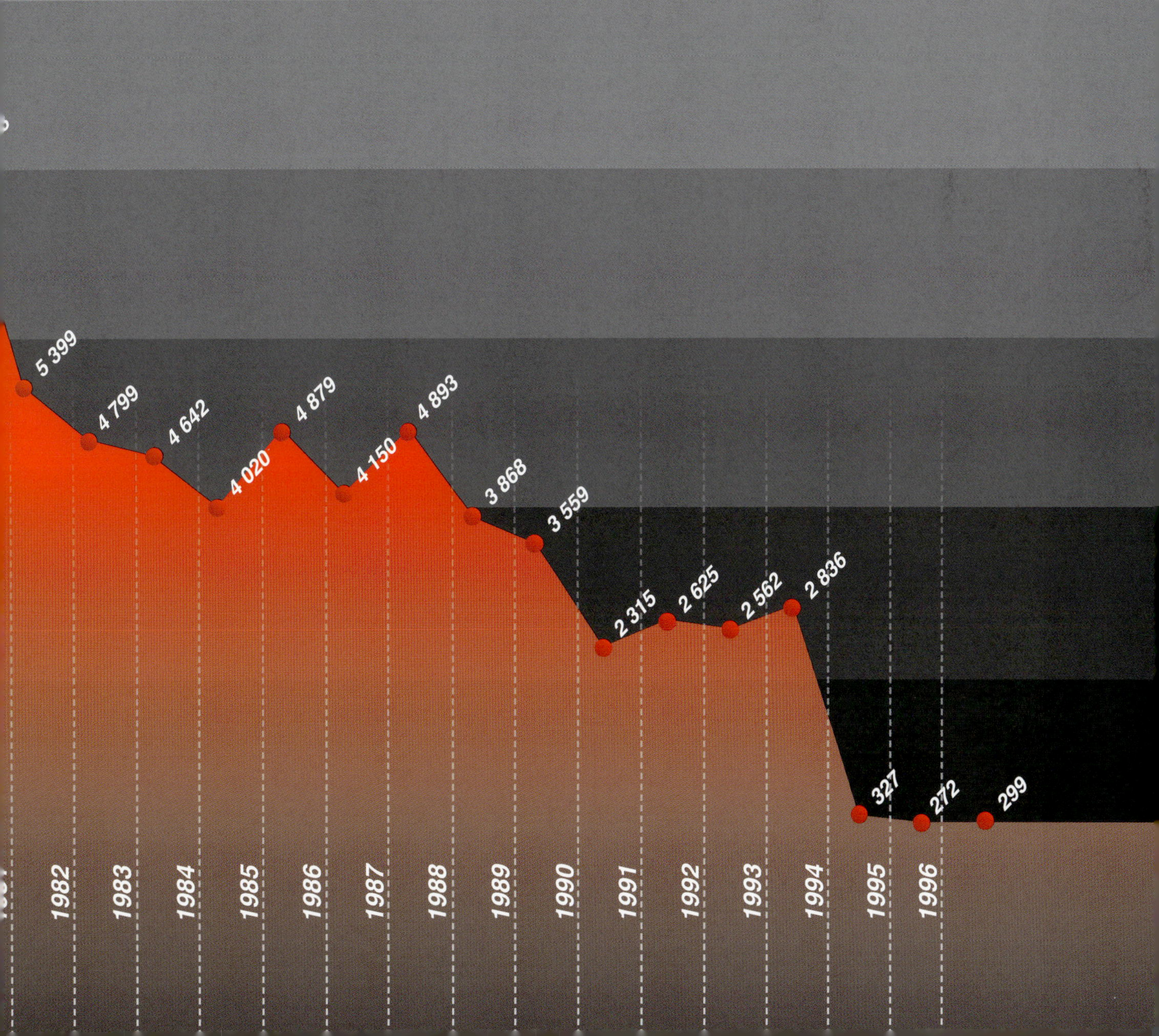

Iconic projects of Zaporizhzhia Modernism

To appreciate the value of Modernist buildings in Zaporizhzhia is impossible without a certain systematisation of its best examples. To appeal to the singular, without having in mind the wider context means to remain forever trapped in artificial hermeneutics. As a historical and cultural phenomenon, Zaporizhzhia Modernism reveals a universal character – one that is free from artificial overloading with meanings taken from local instances – in a developed typology of architectural monuments which outline, together with the contours of their creators' spatial imagination, the social problems of the era.

Departmental palaces of culture, architectural objects for party-Soviet organisations. The departmental palaces of culture and buildings designed for party-Soviet organisations and independent youth movements have, in fact, no direct typological counterparts today: they are already oases of urban historical environment. An understanding of them, along with all the other typical examples of Modernism of the 1960s–80s, will offer considerable potential for forming historical-architectural connections, whose density will further determine how meaningful the city continues to be as a cultural form. Only thus will we break the habit of living in the twilight of our own past, subconsciously blaming ourselves for the lost meaningful unity of the city.

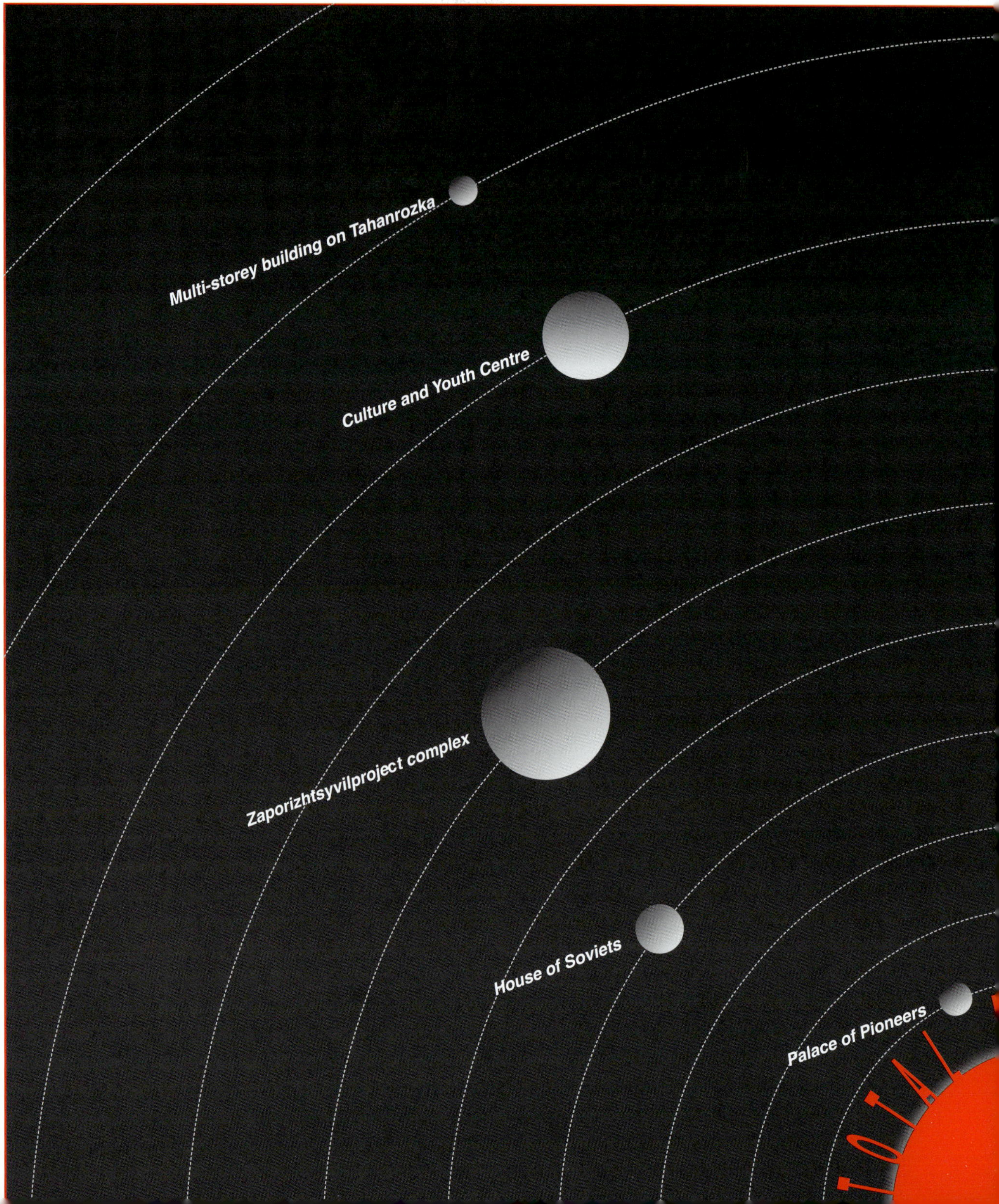
Multi-storey building on Tahanrozka
Culture and Youth Centre
Zaporizhtsyvilproject complex
House of Soviets
Palace of Pioneers
TOTAL

Iconic projects of Zaporizhzhia Modernism

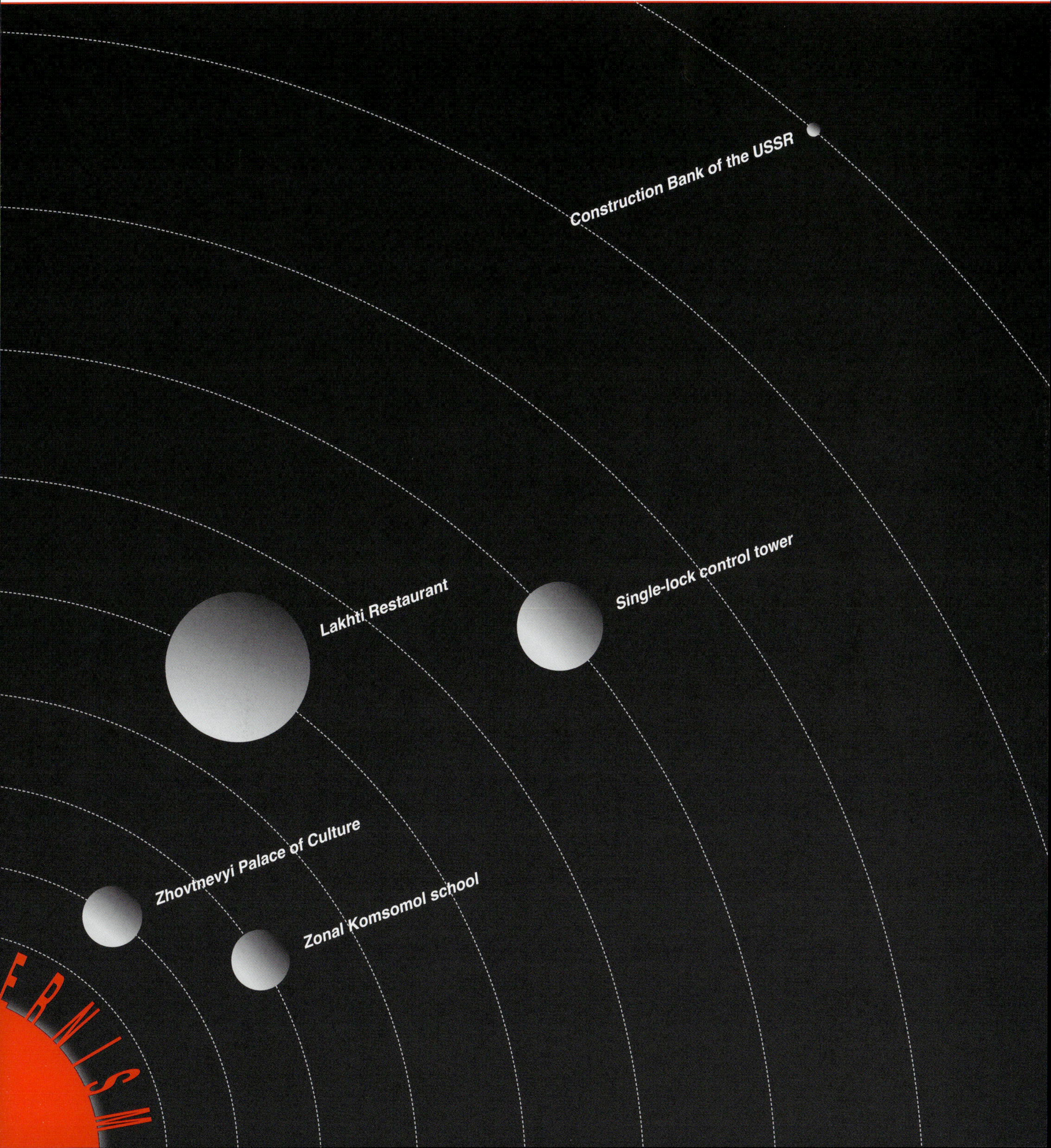

Palace of Pioneers and Schoolchildren, 1986. ***Central Scientific Research Institute for Standardised and Experimental Design of Educational Buildings. Arch.: Drozhzhyn, M.; Sakseltsev, I.; Sorokin, D. Engineers: Anofriiev, V.; Trushyna, L. Decorative design: Bespalov, A.; Zholud O.; Myshevskyi, Ye.; Khomchyk, V.; Shcherbyna, O.***

Zaporizhzhia Square, 1

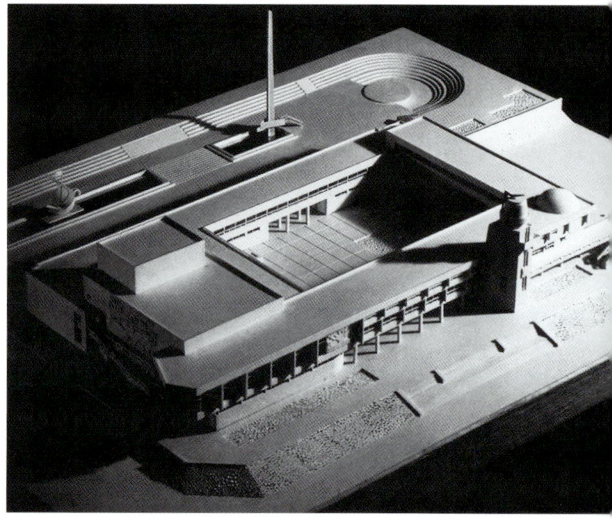

ДОБРО ПОЖАЛОВАТЬ!

Palace of Pioneers and Schoolchildren, 1986

Photo: Oleg Burbovski

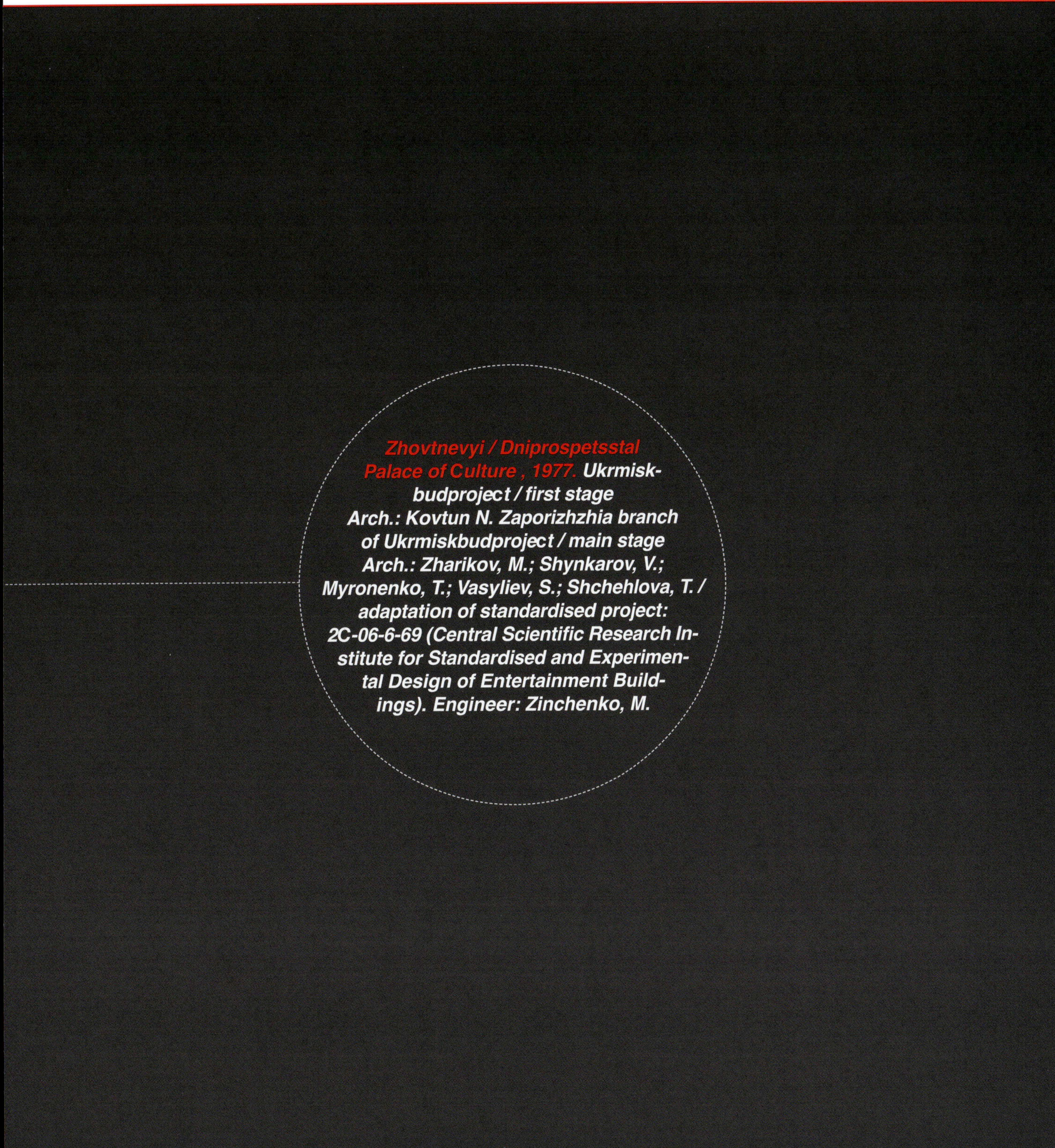

Zhovtnevyi / Dniprospetsstal Palace of Culture , 1977. *Ukrmiskbudproject / first stage Arch.: Kovtun N. Zaporizhzhia branch of Ukrmiskbudproject / main stage Arch.: Zharikov, M.; Shynkarov, V.; Myronenko, T.; Vasyliev, S.; Shchehlova, T. / adaptation of standardised project: 2C-06-6-69 (Central Scientific Research Institute for Standardised and Experimental Design of Entertainment Buildings). Engineer: Zinchenko, M.*

Zhovtnevyi / Dniprospetsstal Palace of Culture, 1977

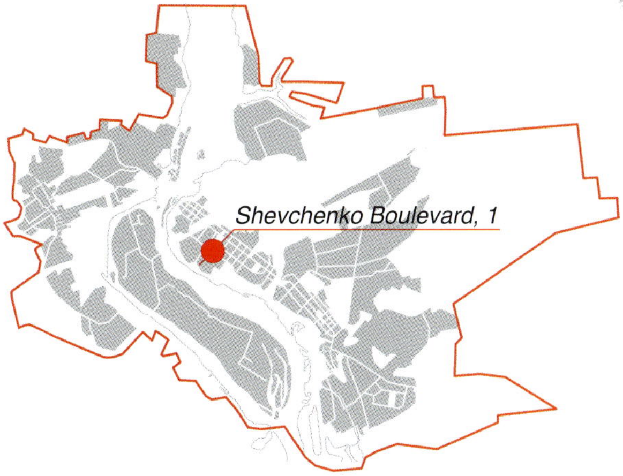

'1. The submitted design brief for the house of culture of the Dniprospetsstal plant is to be approved.

2. The technical council notes that the changes made to the standard project with the approval of the State Construction Committee – the exclusion of the gym, the addition of an indoors swimming pool using inserts and six-metre extensions from the rear façade (from the side of the park) for convenient connection of the club part with the pool and evacuation of the audience, and the adaptation of the façades – are in this particular case justified.

3. When developing working drawings, take into account the following comments: a) when executing the vertical planning project, aim to reduce the retaining wall, steps, and the area abutting the house of culture from the direction of the park; b) plan for green areas, benches, and floor lamps in addition to concrete slabs; c) improve the design of the end façades of the building, remove the entrances, and change the pattern of window openings, arranging them in a functional order; d) reduce the number of entrance steps at the entrances; use light steps; e) for the floors in the building's lobby use mosaic rather than rubber linoleum; f) carefully link all exhaust, ventilation, and other superstructures on the roofs with the architecture of the façades; g) sort out the question of what finishing materials to use for the building's façades and interiors; submit design proposals for the interiors; h) take into account comments made by the fire inspectorate and the client.

4. Note the high architectural performance required by the design brief.'

Extract from the minutes of a meeting of the technical council at the Regional Department for Construction and Architecture (13 June 1967)

Zonal Komsomol school, 1973

Zonal Komsomol school, 1973. Zaporizhzhia branch of Ukrmiskbudproject Arch.: Biriukov, Yu.; Matviienko, A.

Zonal Komsomol school, 1973

House of
Soviets, 1977.
Ukrmiskbudproject
Arch.:
Vasyliev, V.; Yaitskyi, O.;
Nemonov, O.

House of Soviets, 1977

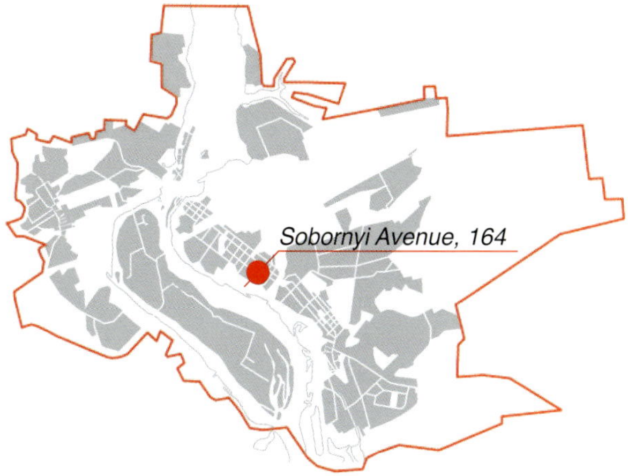

'1. Approve the proposal to place the administrative building for the regional party and Soviet organisations on the central Zhovtneva Square, as provided for by the general plan of the city of Zaporizhzhia.

2. In view of the scale of the area and the surrounding buildings and taking into account the decisive importance of this building in the city's skyline, approve the increase in number of storeys for further development.

3. Further work should be carried out on the detailed model, taking into account the terrain and paying special attention to the development of an architectural and planning solution for a group of multi-storey residential buildings located in the vicinity of Zhovtneva Square [Festyvalna Square] and clearly visible from the Dnipro.

4. Bearing in mind the important position of the specified administrative building in the central part of the city, the difficulty involved in systematically linking its volume with the surrounding buildings, as well as the difficulty of finding a satisfactory architectural and spatial solution, it is recommended to involve 2–3 teams in developing the preliminary design.

5. Feasibility and preliminary-design studies are to be submitted for consideration to the urban-planning and -development department at the Scientific and Technical Council of the State Construction Committee of the Ukrainian SSR.'

Extract from the minutes of a meeting of the urban-planning and -development department of the scientific and technical council of the State Construction Committee of the Ukrainian SSR (3 July 1969)

Restaurant Lakhti, 1973.
Zaporizhzhia branch of Ukrmiskbudproject
Arch.: Zaitsev, L.; Dipaolo, L.; Masiutka, A.
Engineers: Dvornikov, B.; Lunina, V.; Abazopulo, M.

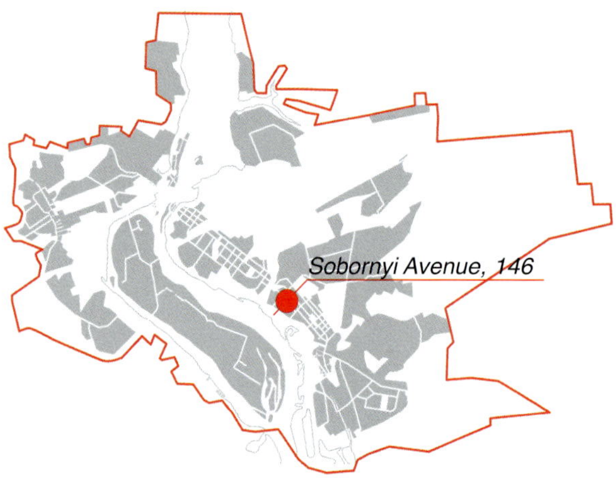
Sobornyi Avenue, 146

Restaurant Lakhti, 1973

The complex of Zaporizhtsyvilproject Design Institute, 1978

The complex of Zaporizhtsyvilproject Design Institute, 1978

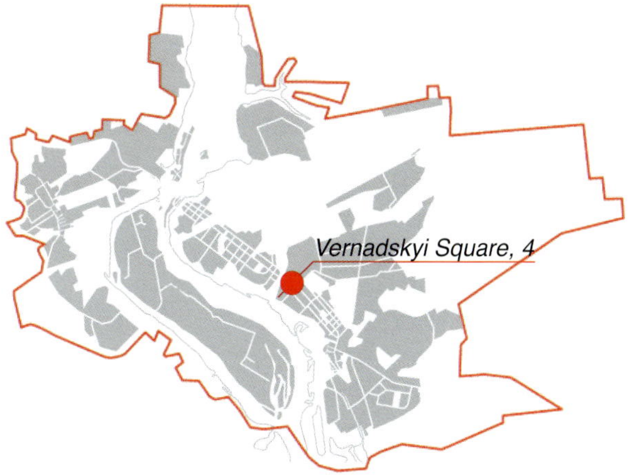

Photo: Maksym Vokhin, 2021

Single-lock control tower, 1980

Single-lock control tower, 1980. **Ukrainian branch of Hydroproject Institute. Arch.: Moshenskyi, A.; Okhrimenko, I.**

Sobornyi Avenue, 240

Single-lock control tower, 1980

Photo: Oleg Burbovski

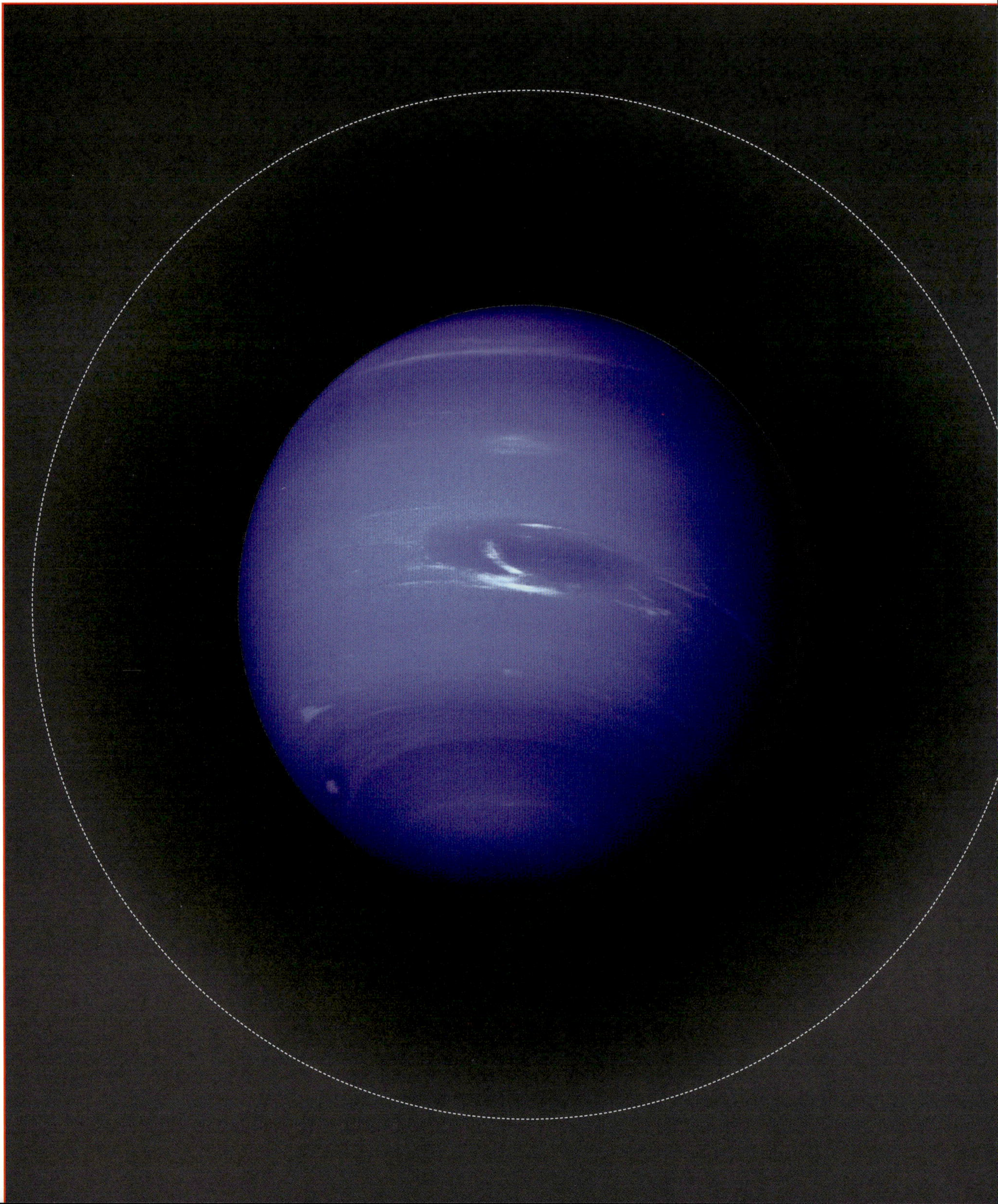

Youth Cultural Centre / House of Political Education, 1988

Youth Cultural Centre / House of Political Education, 1988.
Zaporizhtsyvilproject. Arch.: Shaposhnyk ,V.; Turkovskyi, P. Engineer: Bilinska, L.

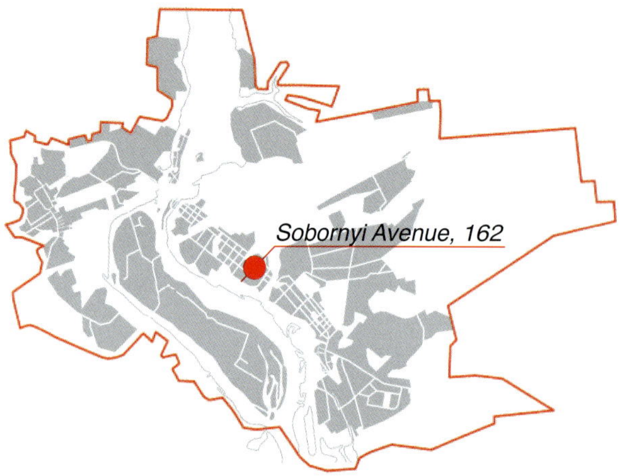
Sobornyi Avenue, 162

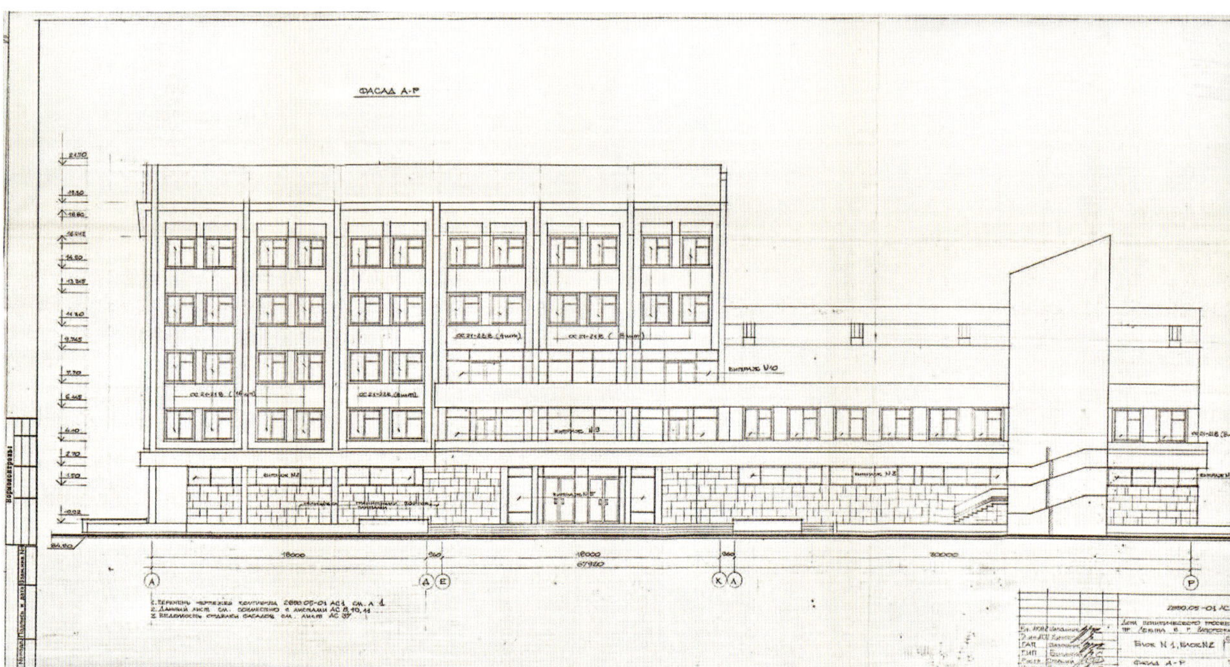
ФАСАД А-Р

Youth Cultural Centre / House of Political Education, 1988

Photo: Dmytro Smolienko, 2022

Restaurant Bezimennyi, 1974

Restaurant Bezimennyi, 1974. Central Scientific Research Institute for Standardised and Experimental Design of Trade and Service Buildings and Tourist Complexes. Arch.: Bikson, E.

РОССИЯ
РОССИЯ

Restaurant Bezimennyi, 1974

Photo: Pavlo Kravchuk, 2023

Photo: Dmytro Smolienko, 2024

Construction Bank, 1978.
Zaporizhzhia branch of Ukrmiskbudproject
Arch.: Zharikov, M.; Shaposhnyk, V.
Engineers: Romanova, T.; Troitska, V.; Liubivaia, N.; Sharfman, M.;Kazakova, M.; Kriachun, M.

Construction Bank, 1978

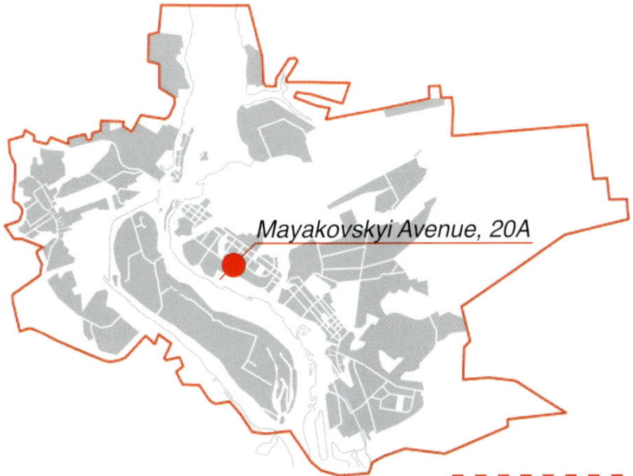

Photo: Mykhailo Mordovskoi, 2022

The apartment as a focus of social transformation

Systematic housing development in the USSR was a historical paradox. On the one hand, it was a form of implementation of national social policy with unifying mechanisms of control over the production of the urban environment and over the reproduction of social activity (in both cases, through uniformity and normativity). On the other hand, the mass production of housing in the form of individual apartments led to an unprecedented increase in private space outside the control of Soviet and trade union organisations. Until the 1960s access to a stable private space had depended on the hierarchical position of the user of the living space in the state management system and in production; this led to learned mechanisms of self-control being transferred into everyday life. The mass provision of individual apartments to strata of the population for whom a place in the management hierarchy made no obvious sense significantly reduced space that was subject to social control. Realised through the homogeneity of systematic micro-district development, the total state vision now stopped at the threshold of individual apartments. Communication practices ('kitchen conversations') were transformed; the culture of sexual life (including through the availability of separate bedrooms) and childhood also changed. The fact that children now grew up with the benefits of private space contributed to the breakdown of the collectivist psychology in educational institutions and to the development of alternative leisure and counterculture. Mass individual-apartment housing became the 'black box' that unbalanced the customary state-controlled course of everyday life and set off social demand and the transition to Soviet pluralism as an instrument in the depoliticisation of public life.

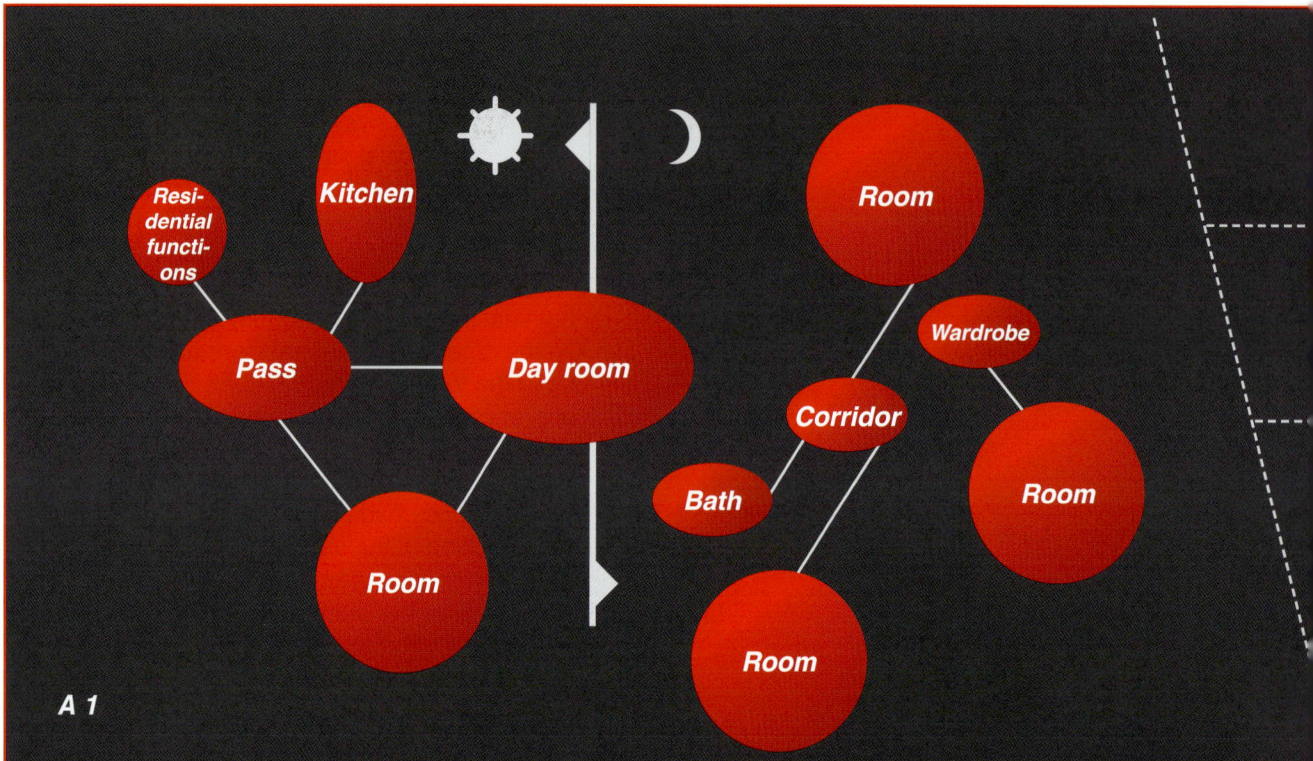
Resi-
dential
functi-
ons
Kitchen
Pass
Day room
Room
Room
Wardrobe
Corridor
Bath
Room
Room

A 1

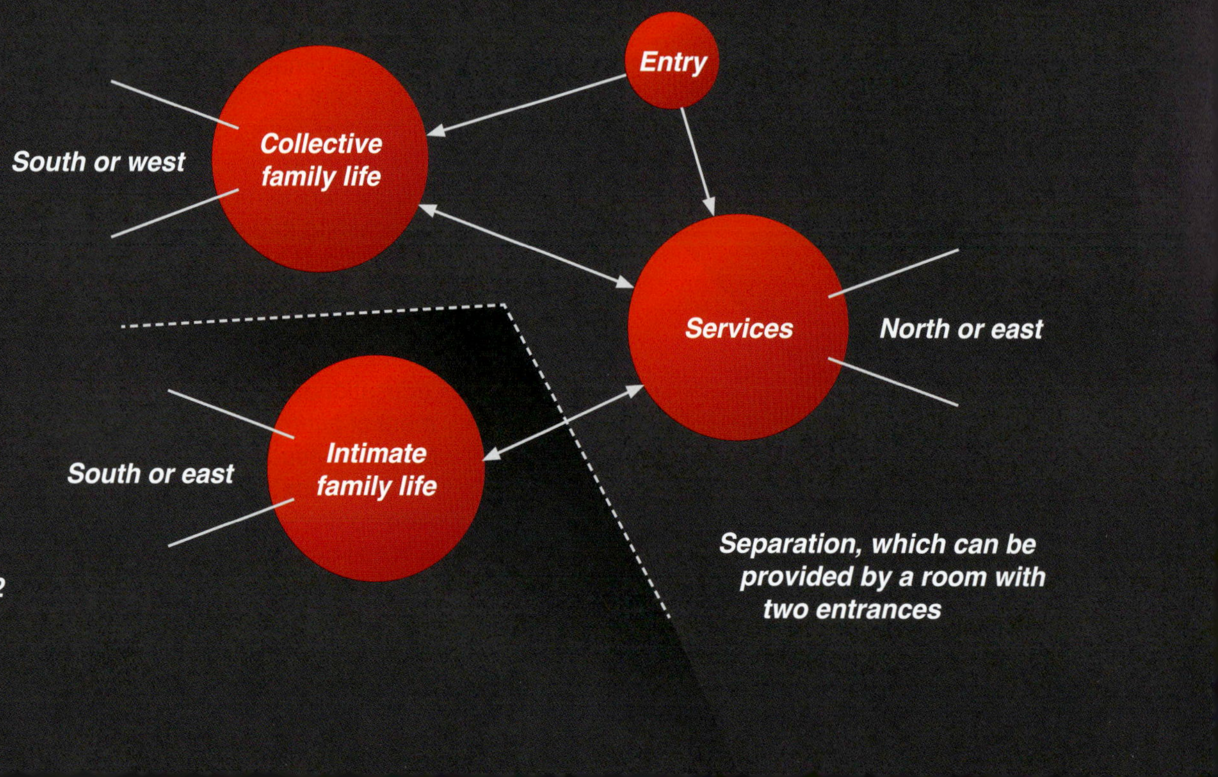
Entry
South or west
Collective
family life
Services
North or east
South or east
Intimate
family life
Separation, which can be
provided by a room with
two entrances

A 2

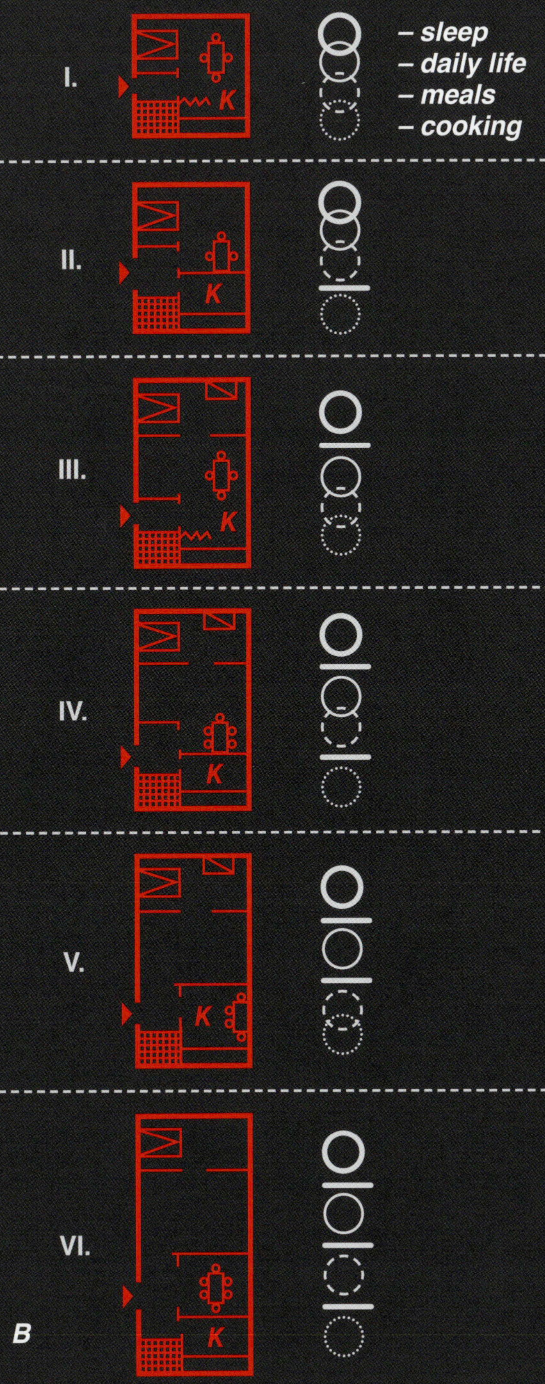

Residential functions of the apartment

A — unification of functions according to the principle of 'day – night' (1) and 'public – private life' (2)

B — methods of laying out the apartment, which determine degree of differentiation of functions;
I — no differentiation
II– IV — partial differentiation
V — complete differentiation

Residential functions of an apartment, from the book 'Basics of Housing Evolution', 1968

cigarette smoke

From 'Secondhand Time: The Last of the Soviets', a book by the Nobel laureate Svetlana Alexievich

'1960s dissident life is kitchen life. Thanks, Khrushchev! He's the one who led us out of the communal apartments; under his rule, we got our own private kitchens where we could criticise the government and, most importantly, not be afraid, because in the kitchen you were always among friends. It's where ideas were whipped up from scratch, fantastical projects concocted. We made jokes — it was a golden age for jokes! "A communist is someone who's read Marx; an anticommunist is someone who's understood him."'[1]

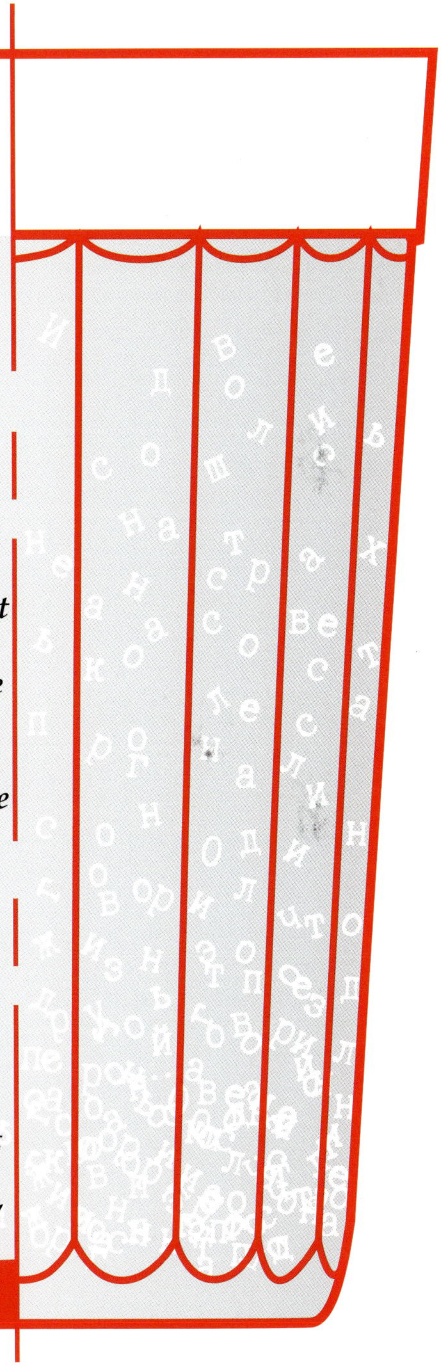

A work at the exhibition 'Modern Soviet Photography', 1987

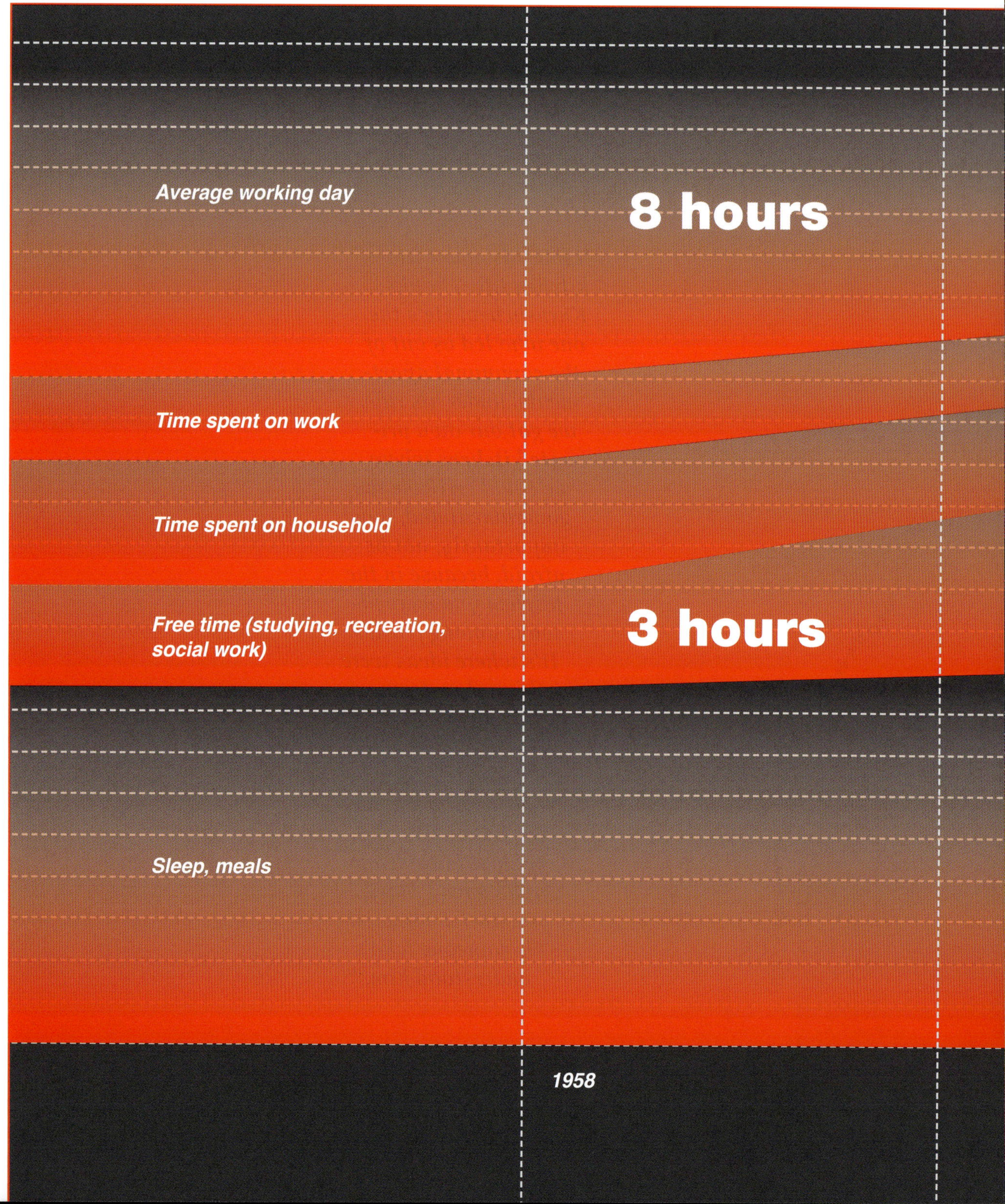
Average working day
8 hours
Time spent on work
Time spent on household
Free time (studying, recreation, social work)
3 hours
Sleep, meals
1958

Late 1950s to 1980s. The progressive impact of spatial transformation on social processes

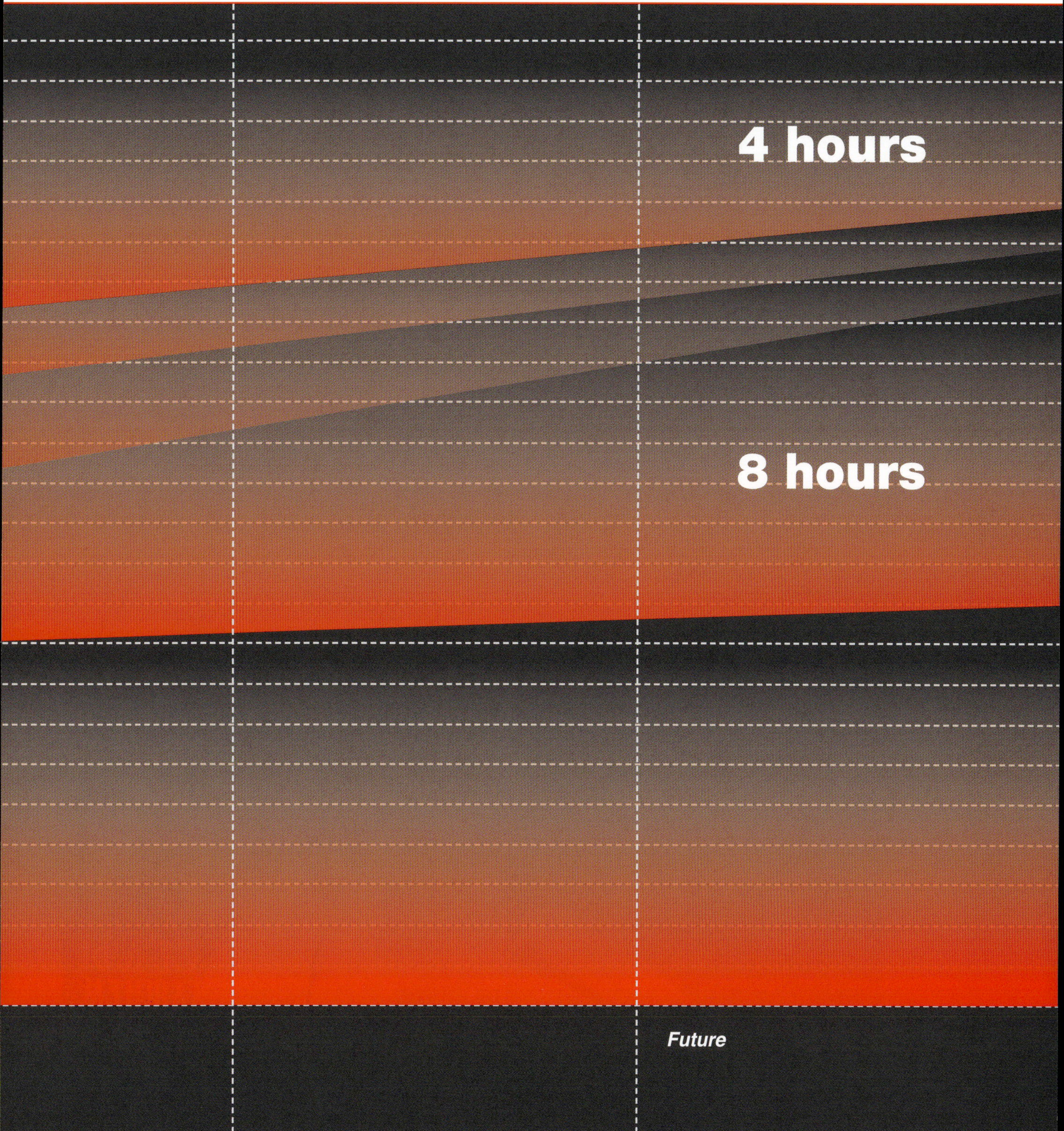

Conversations About the Household (1959), a textbook for people moving to new apartment, was published in an edition of one million copies.

While providing apartments to citizens who had previously lived in collective living conditions and did not know what private space was, the Soviet authorities launched a campaign to explain to the population the proper way to manage their individual apartments. This included the propagation of a new culture of body care, a new culture of consumption, and a new culture of leisure. The leitmotif of this broad campaign was counteracting philistinism and 'shameful' habits centred on private property.

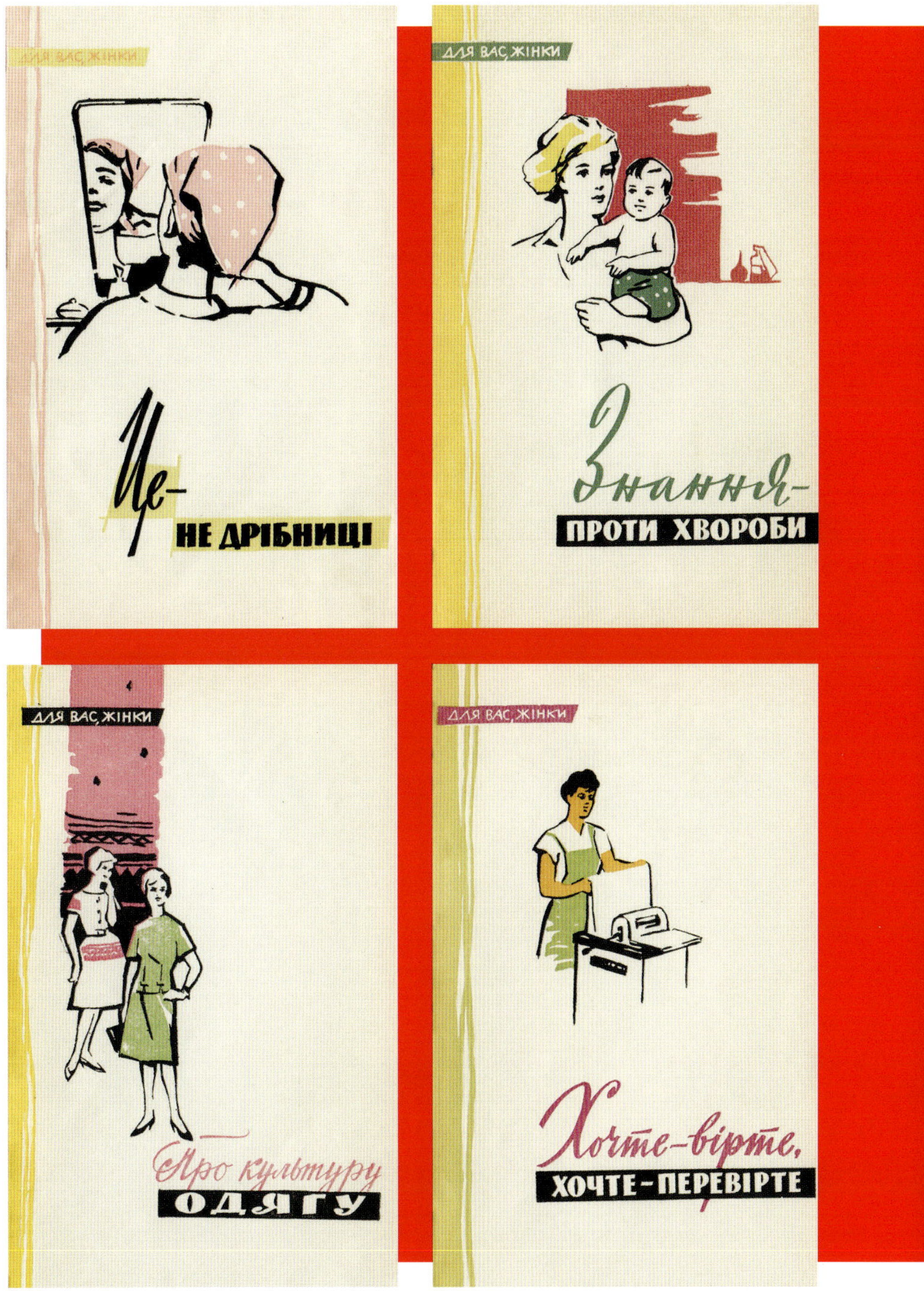

A set of brochures issued by the Znannya Society (1963) informing women about how to live and behave at work and in the home

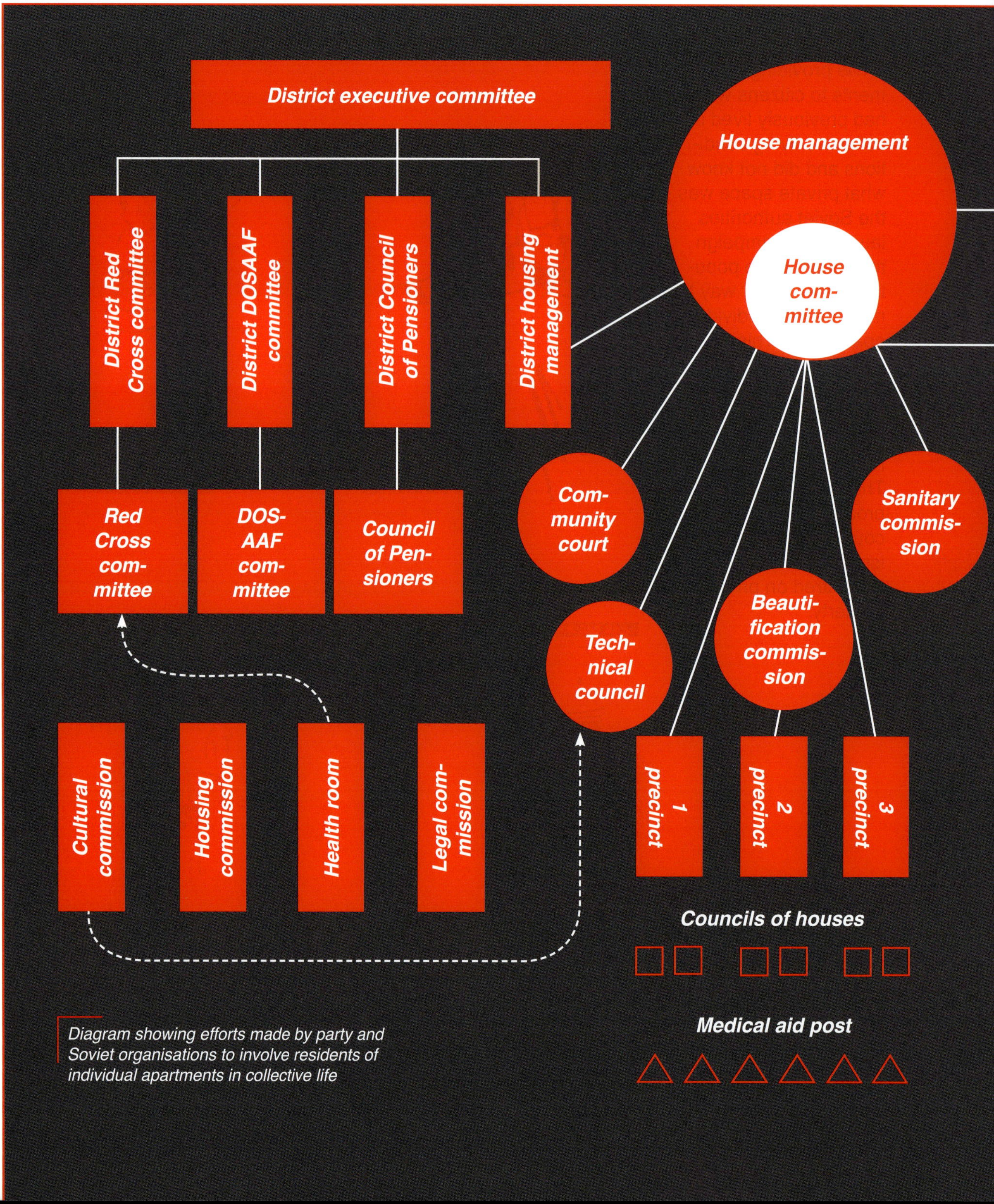

Diagram showing efforts made by party and Soviet organisations to involve residents of individual apartments in collective life

1960s. Attempts by the state to direct processes in individual apartments

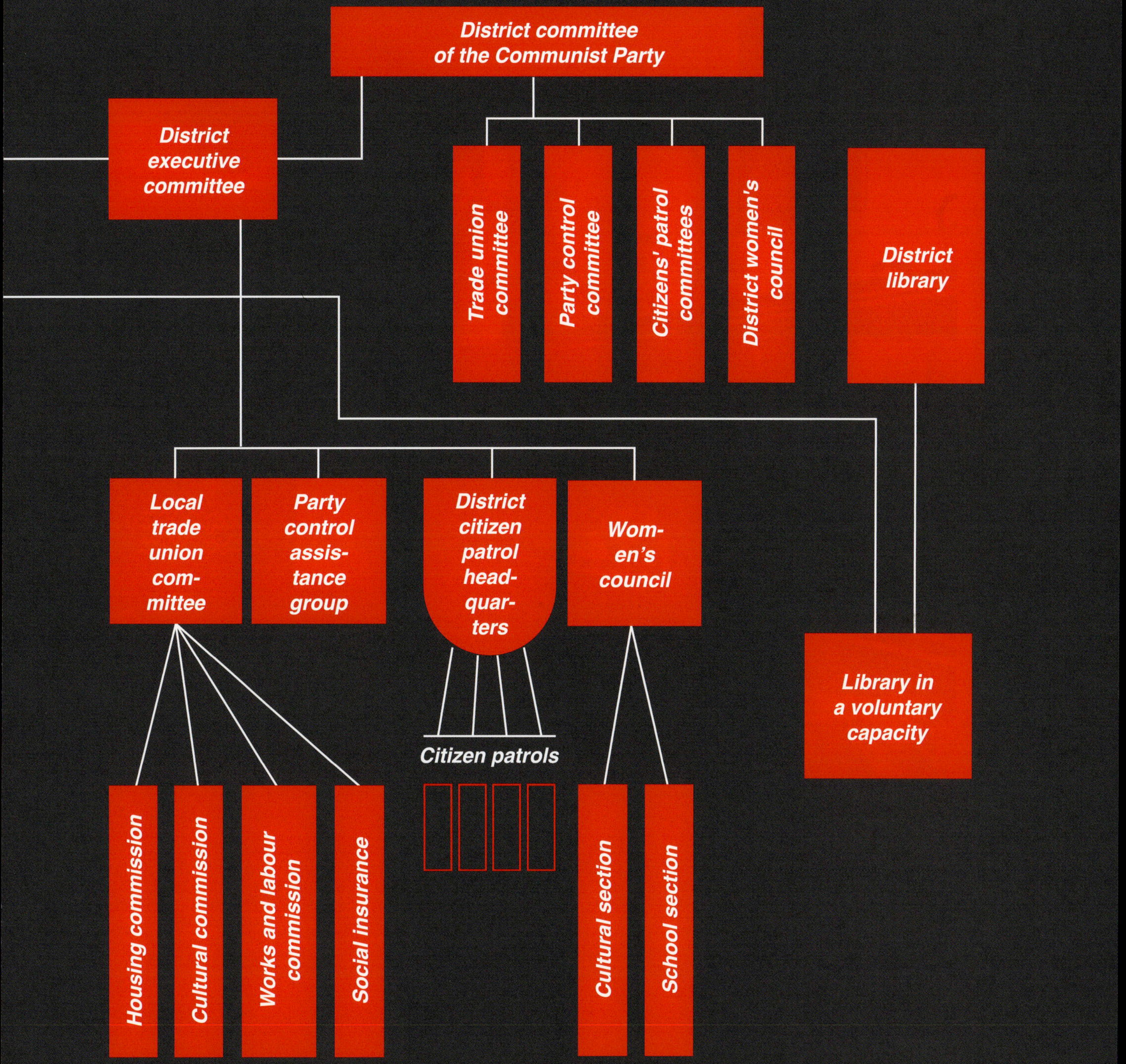

Standard interior of a living room and bedroom. 1979. Micro-district No. 3 in the Dniprobud-II residential area

Growth of housing stock in the city of Zaporizhzhia and average provision of citizens with gross living space, 1941–1986

Parameter	*1941*	*1946*	*1969*	*1981*	*1986*
Public stock (city council, enterprises, institutions), thousand square metres	916.5	384.7	2995.6	7416.6	9350.5
In individual ownership, thousand square metres	864.6	752.0	1460.5	2282.0	2004.0
In cooperative ownership, thousand square metres			281.3	1176.4	1398.5
Total housing stock, thousand square metres	1781.1	1136.7	4737.4	10,875	12,753
Population of Zaporizhzhia, thousands of people	360.0	204.4	658.6	812.4	862.9
Average total living area per person, square metres	4.9475	5.56115	7.19314	13.3863	14.7792

Residential building in the Khortytskyi residential area

'By 2000 it is intended to provide practically every Soviet family with separate housing – an apartment or an individual house.'

From a black-and-white projection slide titled 'To the youth, about the CPSU Programme', 1986. Artist: T. Noskova

Transformation of consumer practices

The individual, separate way of life that resulted from people moving to individual apartments and the liberation of households' time budget due to the proximity of service enterprises and the elimination of communal issues such as heating, water supply, and sewage, created a new spatial-temporal continuum of consumption. First, the mass apartment, free of the inevitable sanitary risks involved in maintaining barracks-type or shared (rented) housing in old houses, created a demand for a new hygienic environment (detergents, cosmetics, underwear). Second, food storage and cooking were no longer a matter of communal compromise with neighbours (with stoves, shelves, and tables assigned to different neighbours in the limited space of a shared kitchen). Third, having one's own individual space, usually larger and cleaner than in communal housing, encouraged the renewal of wardrobes, household goods, and, in general, various forms of accumulation. Fourth, with its accompanying larger amount of free time and freedom from neighbourly supervision, the private apartment became a place of leisure (one of the locations of the entertainment industry – reading, listening, watching). Soviet planning authorities and design organisations not only understood the significance of these changes to the household for the nature and scope of mass demand but also tried to streamline the entire consumption system. There was growth in the production and quality of light-industrial goods

and household appliances, which explains the failure of local enterprises in Zaporizhzhia to fulfil the plan for individual tailoring and repair of appliances in 1961. The postwar standards for provision of residential areas with retail facilities were revised, new standards were approved, and the range of such facilities was expanded (by joint order of the USSR State Trade and Construction Committee in 1965). Standardised architectural and planning solutions were proposed for placing household items and furniture in apartments, including the widespread use of furniture as partitions. However, the mass switch to housing in individual apartments led to unexpected results. The manyfold increase in household consumption and leisure time resulted in a much more complex structure of demand for goods and services and its increasing individualisation to accommodate ideas formed by mass art forms, including foreign cinema, Soviet films about the life of the creative and industrial elite, and colourful magazines from the people's democracies, etc. It was, in fact, systematic housing development that led to the birth of consumer society in the Soviet Union. The competitive pressure of millions of individual households, where well-being was determined by the ability to buy a newer, better-quality item or a larger range of goods, ultimately crushed the command economy with its focus on savings and norms of distribution and use.

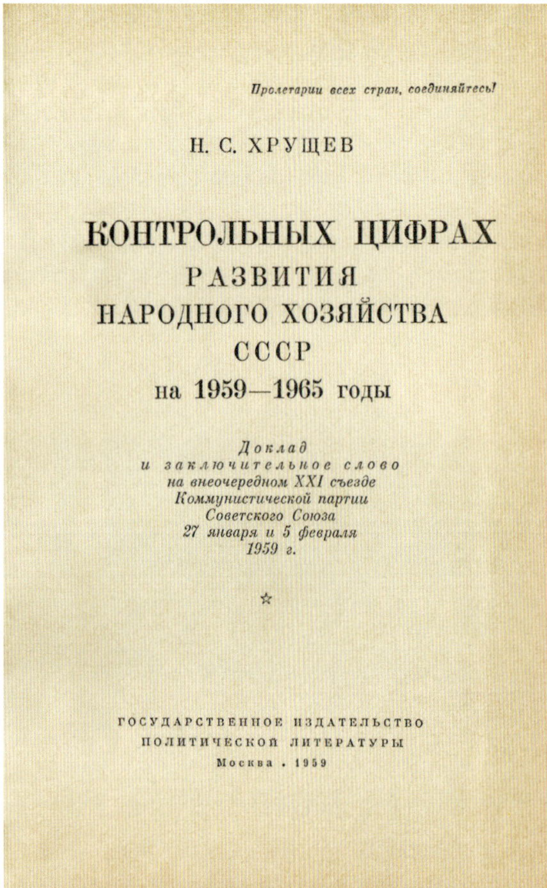

Пролетарии всех стран, соединяйтесь!

Н. С. ХРУЩЕВ

КОНТРОЛЬНЫХ ЦИФРАХ
РАЗВИТИЯ
НАРОДНОГО ХОЗЯЙСТВА
СССР
на 1959—1965 годы

Доклад
и заключительное слово
на внеочередном XXI съезде
Коммунистической партии
Советского Союза
27 января и 5 февраля
1959 г.

☆

ГОСУДАРСТВЕННОЕ ИЗДАТЕЛЬСТВО
ПОЛИТИЧЕСКОЙ ЛИТЕРАТУРЫ
Москва . 1959

Benchmarks for the Development of the USSR's National Economy for 1959–1965 (Khrushchev's report to the XXI Congress of the Communist Party, 27 January and 5 February 1959).

'The seven-year plan provides for:
– a significant increase in national income and, on this basis, a serious increase in citizens' real incomes;
– reduction of the working day and the number of working days per week;
– increase in the production of consumer goods and improvement of their quality;
– wide-scale housing construction;
– significant improvement of public, cultural, and household services.'

Khrushchev's turbo-programme to improve citizens' welfare

'Sales of cultural and household goods are increasing: refrigerators, washing machines, vacuum cleaners, sewing machines, musical instruments, shoes, garments, knitwear, silk fabrics, food products, and other goods. To ensure fulfilment of the turnover plan, it is planned to open 41 stores with 147 jobs and 58 catering establishments with 2248 seats, including: 26 canteens, two 200-seat restaurants, eight home kitchens, ten culinary shops, etc."

From the report on the state plan for the development of the economy of the city of Zaporizhzhia for 1961

On 24 July 1959 an impromptu series of dialogues between Nikita Khrushchev, the Soviet leader, and Richard Nixon, the US vice president, took place at the American Exhibition in Moscow. These conversations, known as 'the kitchen debates', helped redefine the social role of Soviet citizens as active consumers.

The real level of satisfaction of the population's needs for services, non-food goods, and food goods (Labour Research Institute, 1967)

Actual provision

Normative provision

Khrushchev’s turbo-programme to improve citizens’ welfare

	Paid services	*Non-food goods*	*Food goods*
	20%	25%	67%
	100%	100%	100%

9000 inhabitants; R = 400 m. (optimal)

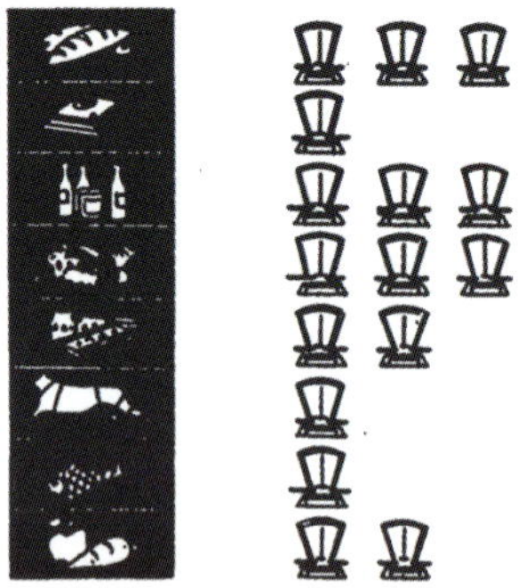

Total of **16** work-places

Cost of one workplace **100 %**

1280 students
In future: 960 students
Network of educational and auxiliary premises:
- 5 laboratories
- sports hall, 12 × 24 m.
- assembly hall, 12 × 24 m.
- dining room, 288 sq. m.

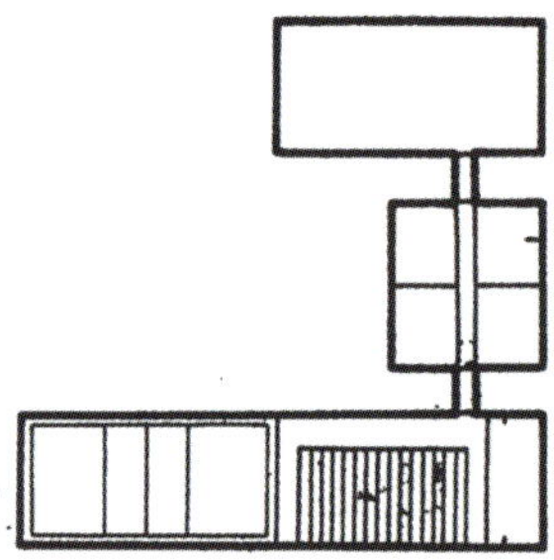

Cost of one student place **100 %**

Universal hall, 15 × 30 m.
550 seats

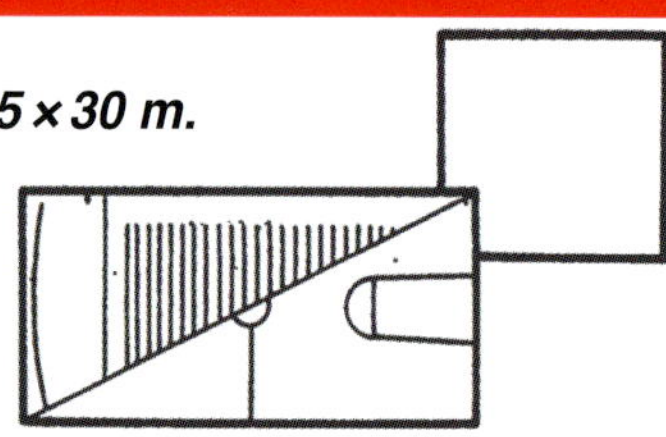

Types of sessions:

Cost of one spectator seat **100 %**

6000 inhabitants; R = 350 m.

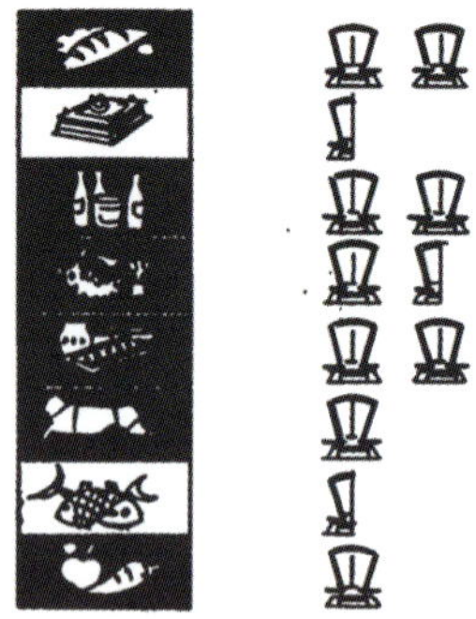

Total of **11** work-places

Cost of one workplace **106 %**

960 students
In future: 720 students
Network of educational and auxiliary premises:
- 3 laboratories
- sports hall, 12 × 24 m.
- assembly hall/buffet, 210 sq. m.

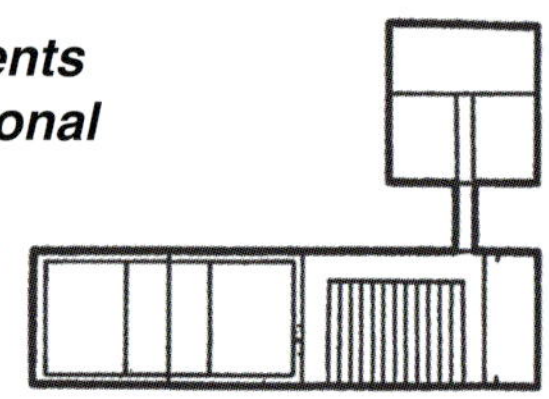

Cost of one student place **110 %**

Universal hall, 12 × 24 m.
330 seats

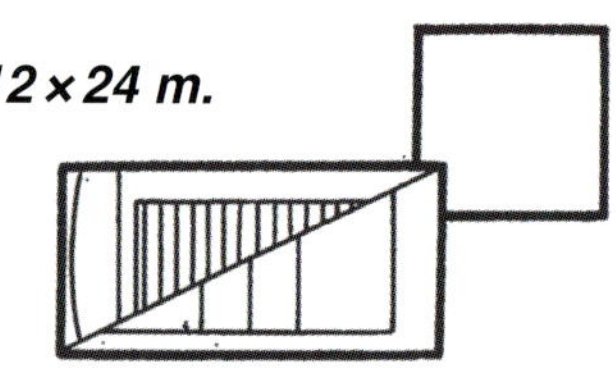

Types of sessions:

Cost of one spectator seat **117 %**

4000 inhabitants; R = 300 m. (not recommended)

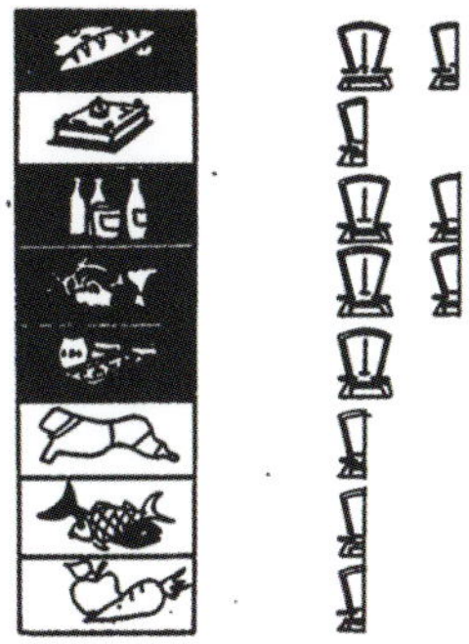

Total of
6
work-places

Cost of one workplace 114 %

640 students
In future: 720 students
Set of educational and auxiliary premises:
- 3 laboratories
- sports hall 9 × 18 m.
- assembly hall/buffet, 140 sq. m.

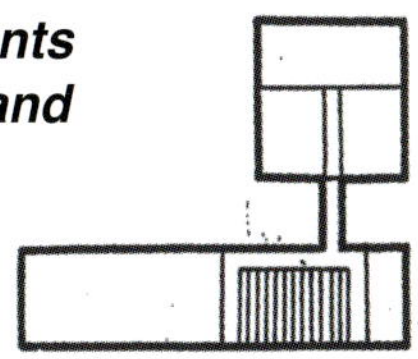

Cost of one student place 127 %

Universal hall 9 × 18 m
200 seats

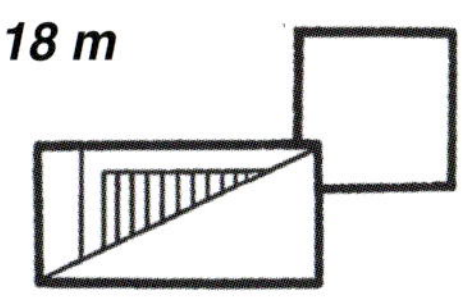

Types of sessions:

Cost of one spectator seat 124 %

Comparison of the cost of service networks, depending on number of people and radius of operation (author: Heorhii Hradov, 1968)

Cosmos Cinema (1968), a standardised design project for a large-format cinema with 600 seats (1c-06-15), developed by the Mosoblproiekt Institute in 1965, adapted by the Zaporizhzhia branch of Ukrmiskbudproekt

Design proposal for a public and shopping centre in the old city (Malyi Rynok), first half of the 1970s. Central Scientific Research Institute for Standardised and Experimental Design of Trade and Service Buildings and Tourist Complexes. Architect: Eduard Bikson

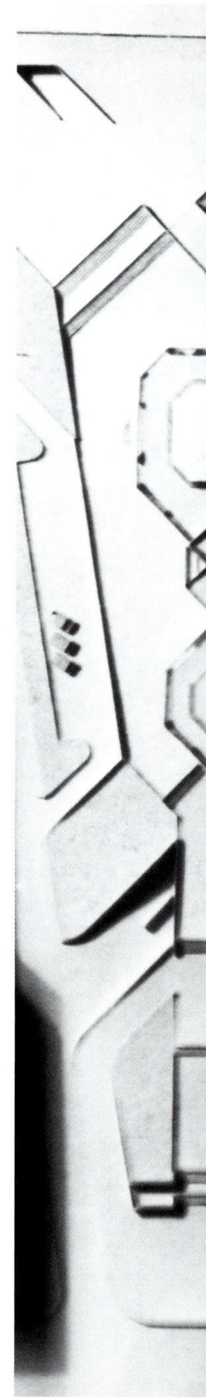

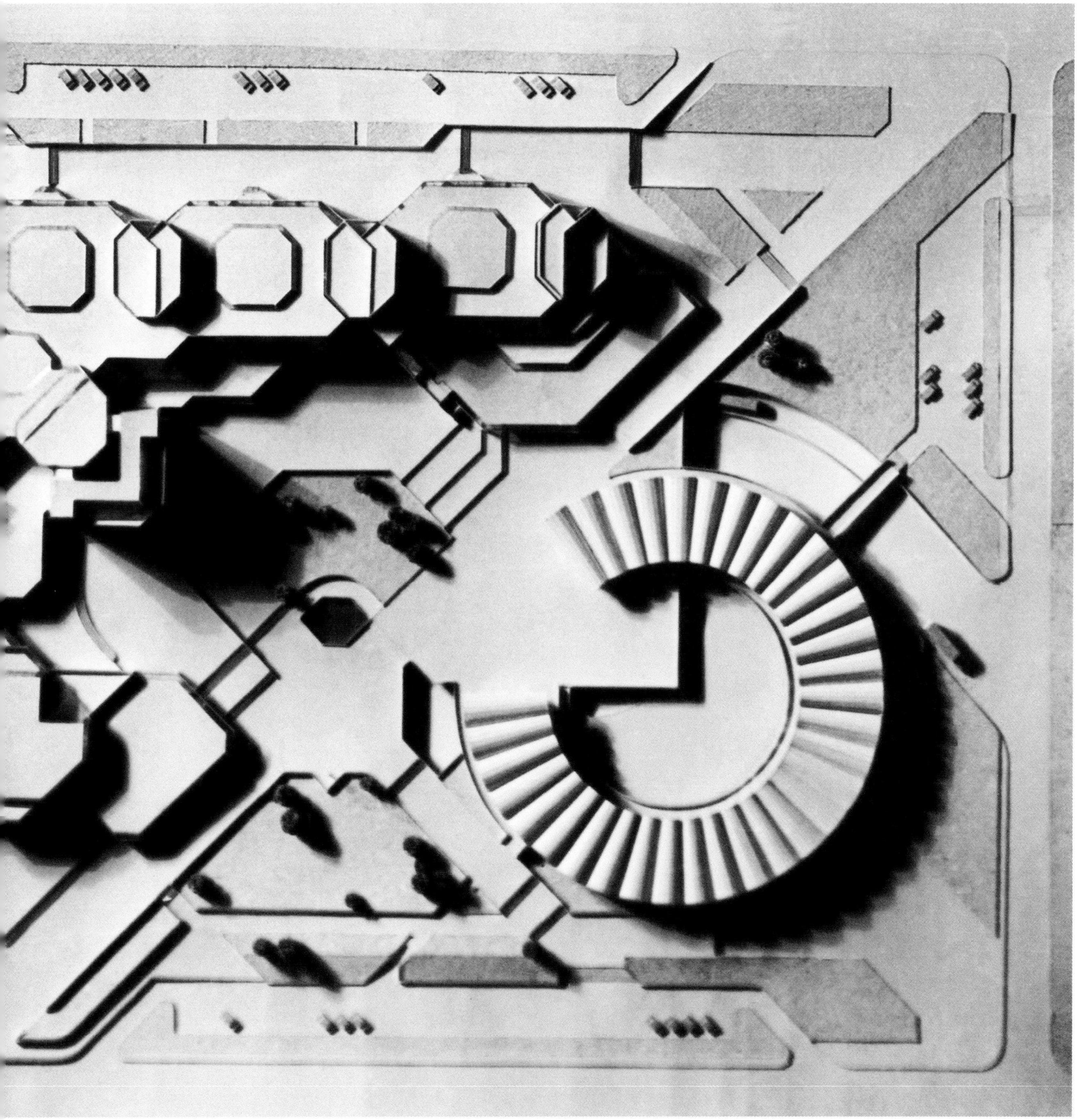

Plan 'K'

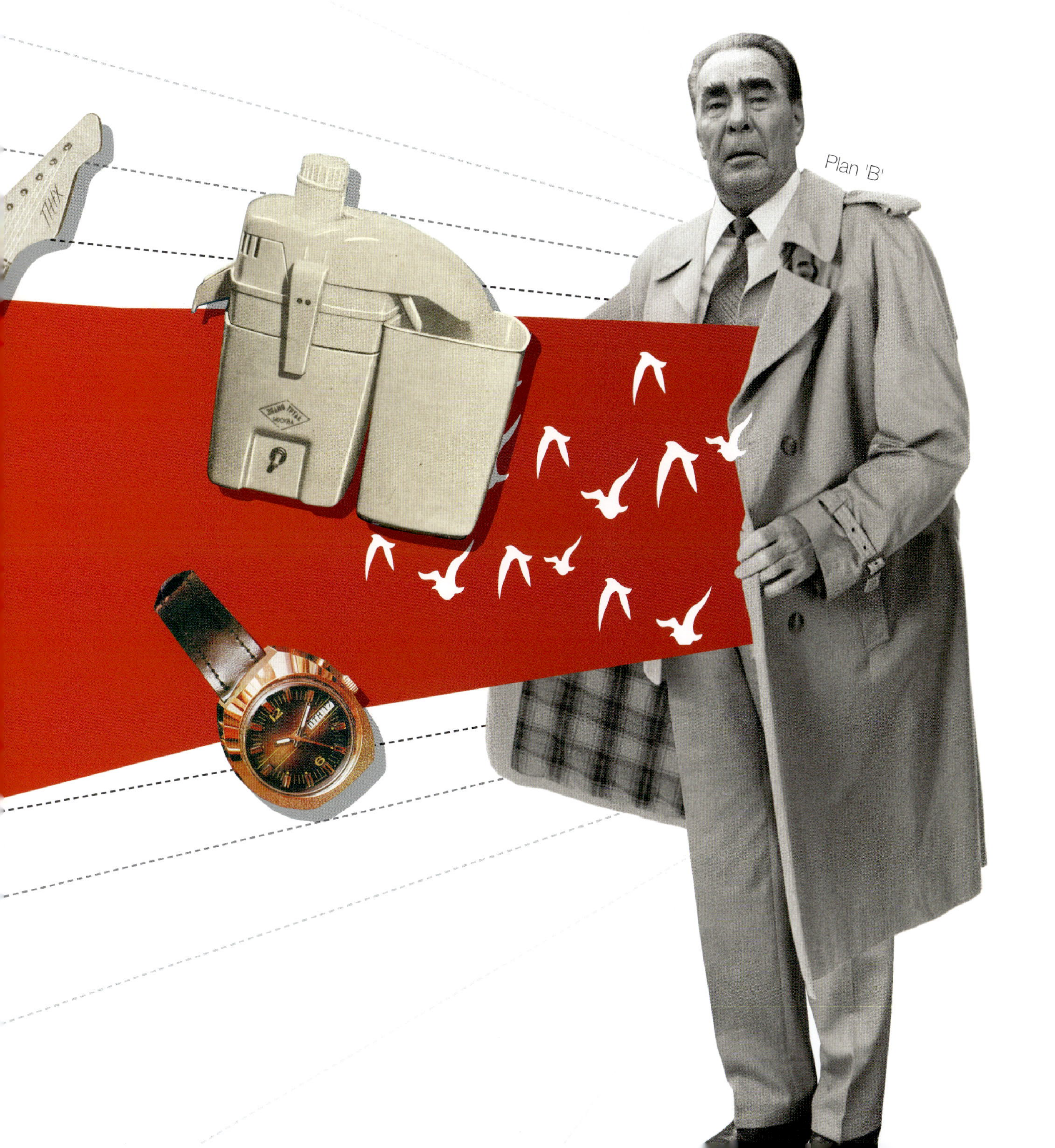
Plan 'B'

Plan 'G'

Architecture of urban-planning ensembles

In 1957 – 1958 the Urban-Planning Research Institute of the Academy of Construction and Architecture of the Ukrainian SSR drew up basic provisions and design proposals for the development of the central part of Zaporizhzhia. These were approved by the USSR State Construction Committee in 1959. On the basis of this urban-planning documentation, a team consisting of S. Vasylevskyi (chief architect of the city), H. Vehman (Ukrmiskbudproject Design Institute), A. Ivanova, and H. Orekhova (Urban-Planning Research Institute of the USSR Academy of Construction and Architecture) developed a layout for Zaporizhzhia's Central District, including a main city centre with a plan showing the placement of institutions. The centre was designed to be a traffic-free, pedestrian boulevard. Public service institutions were to be located along this boulevard. An alternative proposal made by Dipromisto placed the main square and the Palace of Councils south of Sobornyi Avenue (currently on the north side): 'Placing the square here with its buildings open towards the south will make it clearly visible from the Dnipro. This option is the best way to ensure that large masses of people can be evacuated from the square to the adjacent streets and creates a direct exit to the park of culture and recreation.' The promenade in the city centre was supposed to connect the main square with the Dnipro embankment and the park zone, where service institutions for the entire city population were located. The amendment of the city's general plan in 1963 led to revision of design proposals for the city centre.

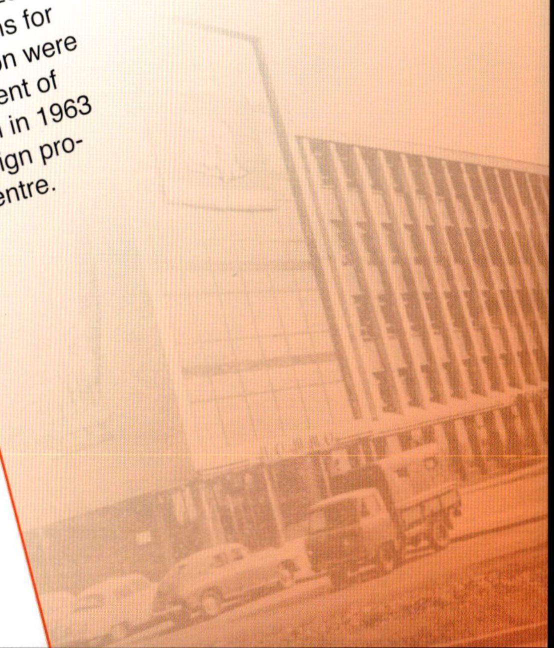

More interesting were the alternative proposals put forward by Ukrmiskbudproject (H. Vehman, N. Kovtun, N. Minakova, E. Belman) and developed in 1960–1961. The centre was designed as an enfilade of three squares situated along a single axis. These are now Festyvalna, Heroiiv, and Trade Unions squares. The Palace of Councils, the focal point of this layout, was located on the highest point north of Sobornyi Avenue on Heroes' Square. During further discussion of Ukrmiskbudproject's proposals at the State Construction Committee and the regional technical council, it was decided to abandon the use of axial symmetry as the basis for the composition – an approach which had been characteristic of the previous stage in the development of national architecture.

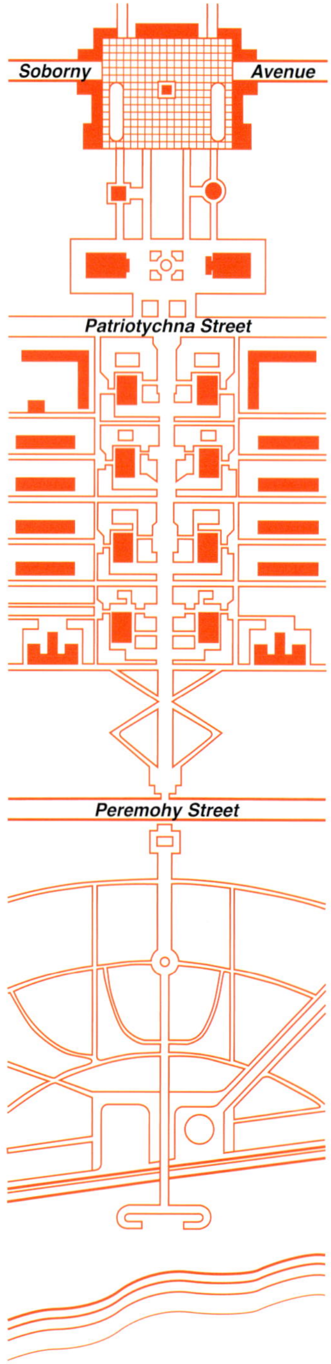

Layout proposal for the city centre, 1959

The issue of access to the water surface of the Dnipro was considered the following year. The architectural and planning brief approved by the USSR State Construction Committee in 1964 (V. Orekhov was one of the developers of the general plan for Great Zaporizhzhia) stipulated that in the waterfront area of the Central District, between the Central Boulevard and Aluminivia Balka, a granite embankment, descents to the Dnipro, street furniture, beaches, a park area, water stations, and parking for day cruisers and private boats were to be designed, and 'in the red water area a botanical garden was to be created.'

Central Blvd.: revision of the classical principles of the urban-planning ensemble

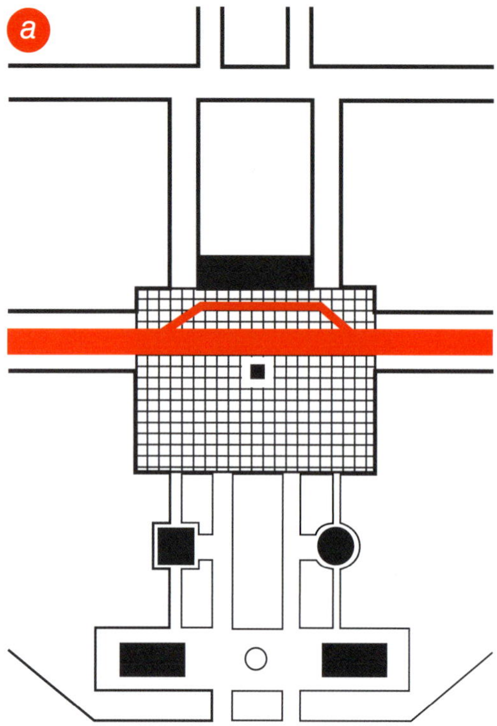

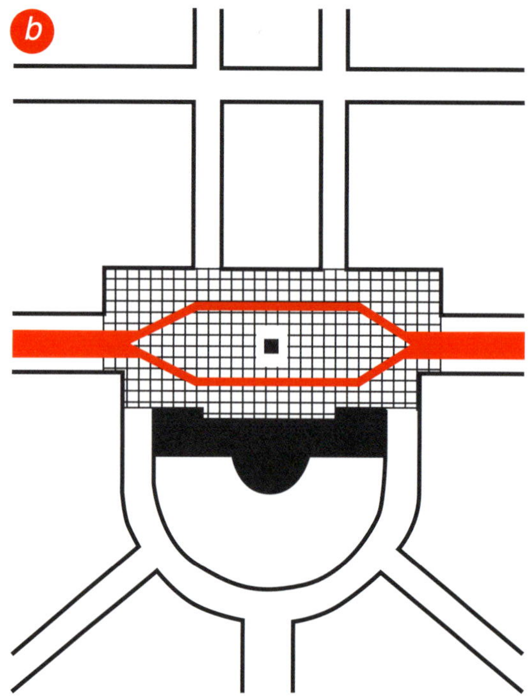

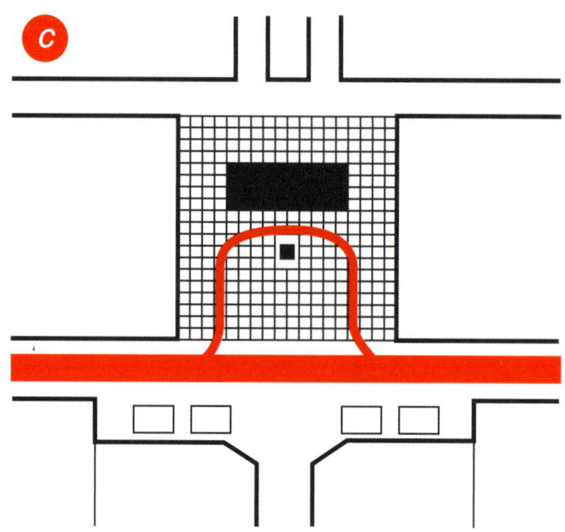

Options for placement of the Palace of Councils in relation to the main avenue and the traffic scheme of the city's public transport in 1959:
a – Urban-Planning Research Institute of the USSR Academy of Construction and Architecture
b – Dipromisto
c – Ukrmiskbudproject

Central Blvd.: revision of the classical principles of the urban-planning ensemble

Layout of the development of Central Boulevard, 1970

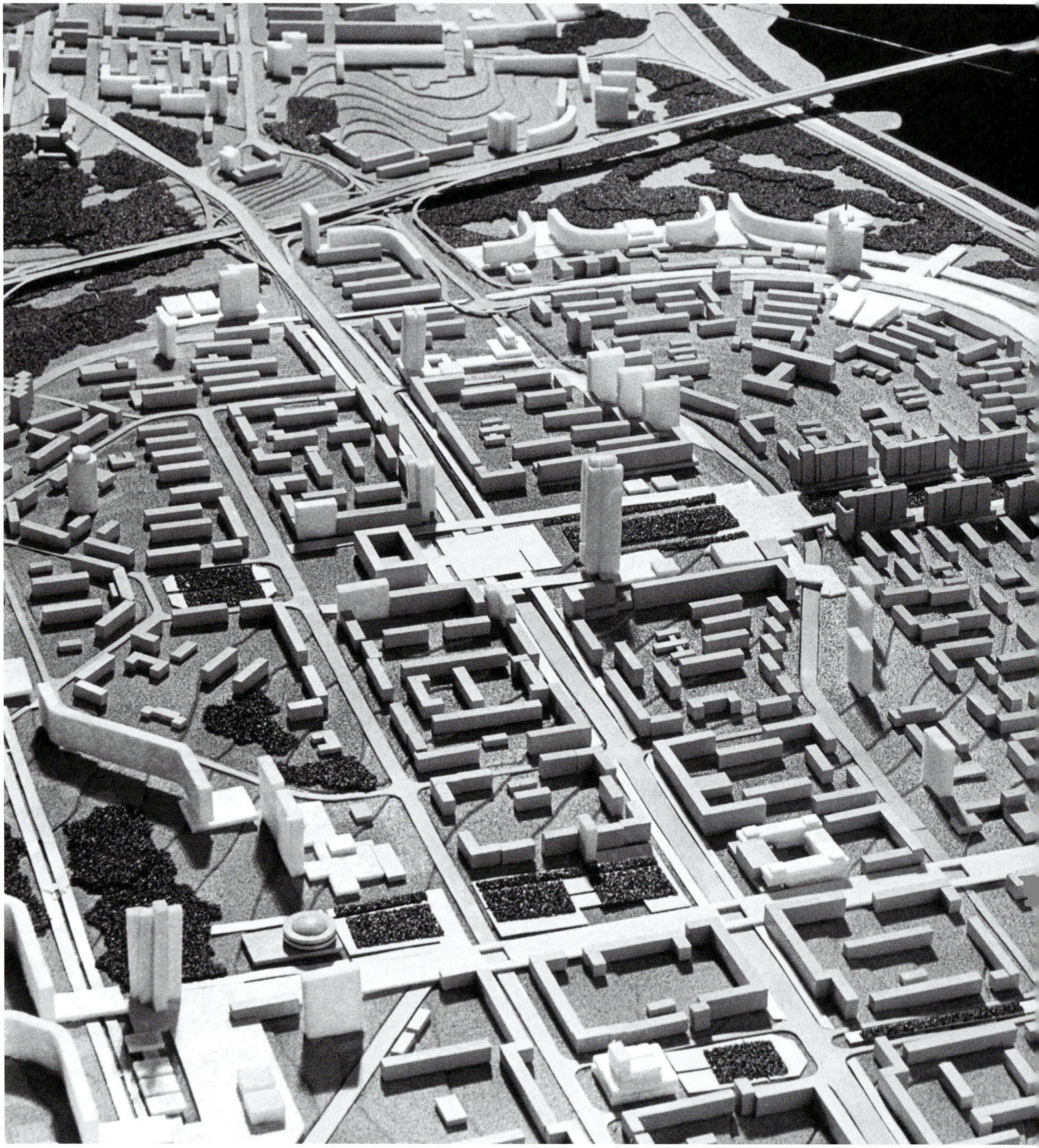

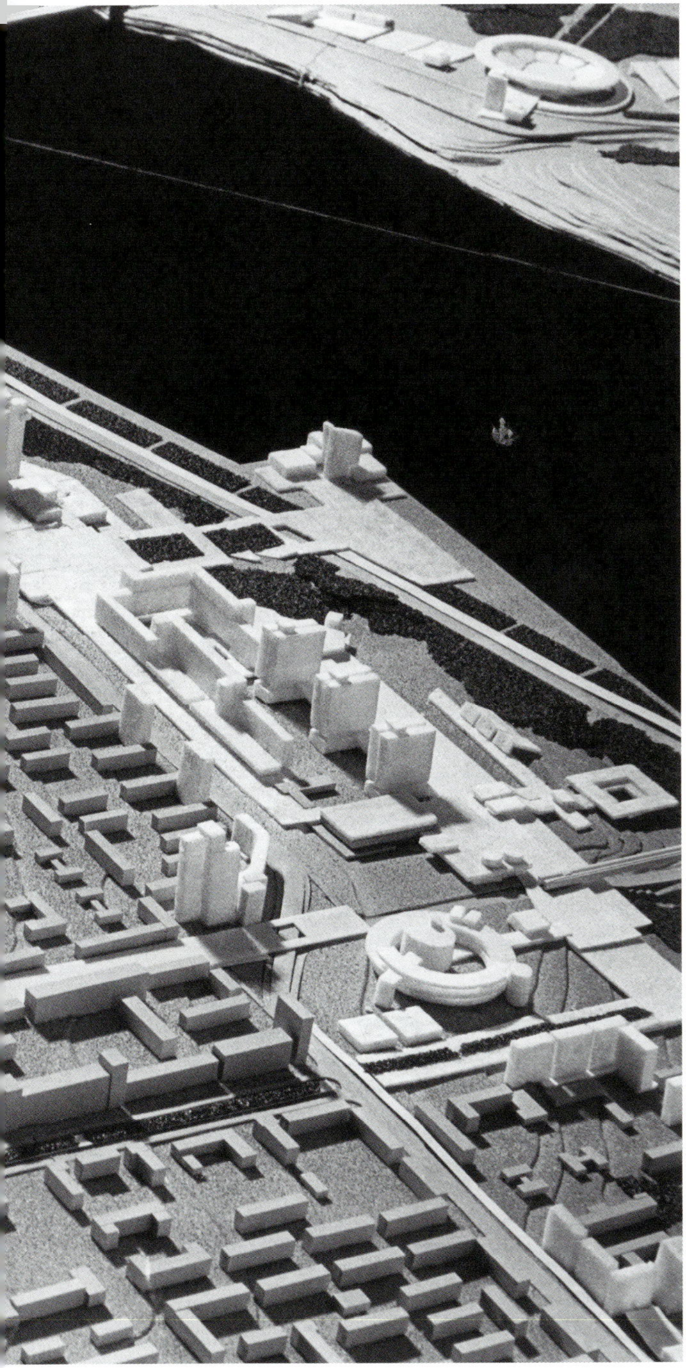

Layout of the central part of the city, early 1970s

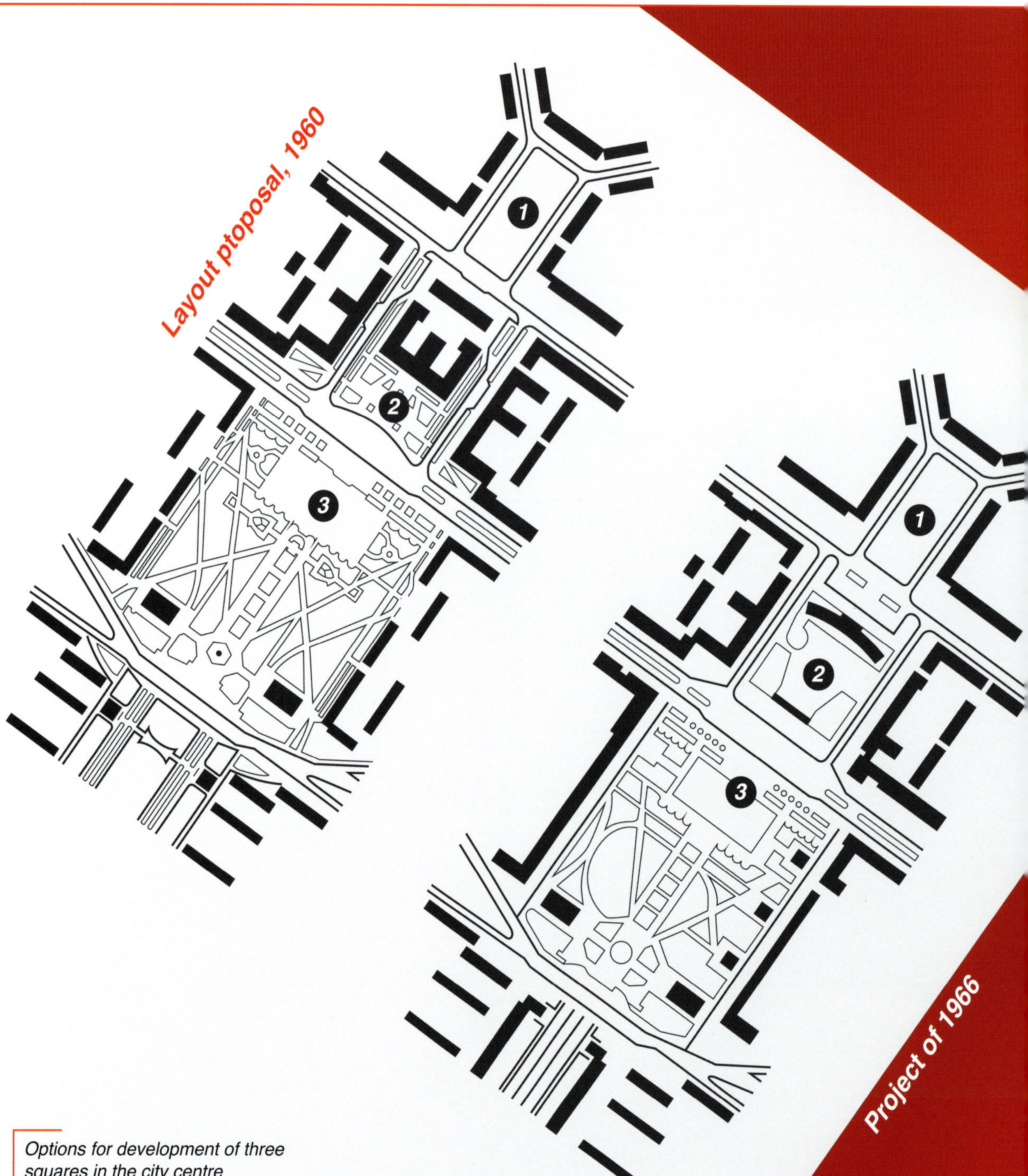

Options for development of three squares in the city centre

Central Blvd.: revision of the classical principles of the urban-planning ensemble

1. Trade Unions Square
2. Zhovtneva Square (Heroiiv)
3. Festyvalna Square

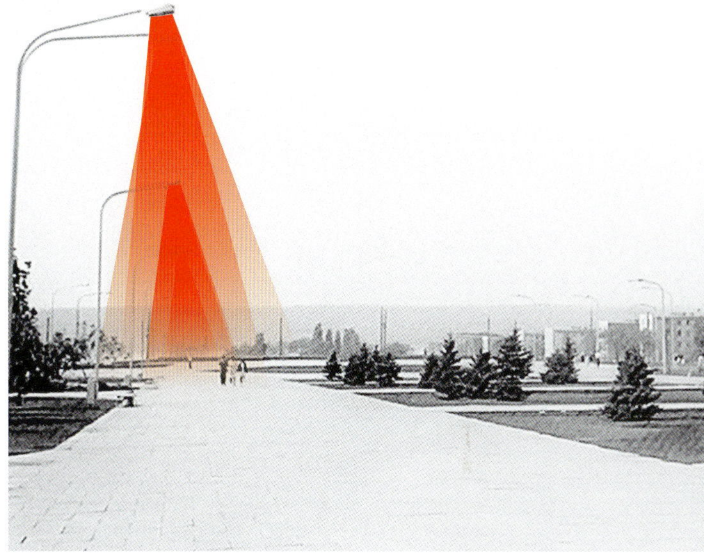

At the corner of Central Boulevard and Patriotychna Street, 1970s

Central Boulevard, 1980s

The proposal for the development of Central Boulevard is demonstrated to honorary citizens of Zaporizhzhia, 1970, photo by O. Burbovskyi.

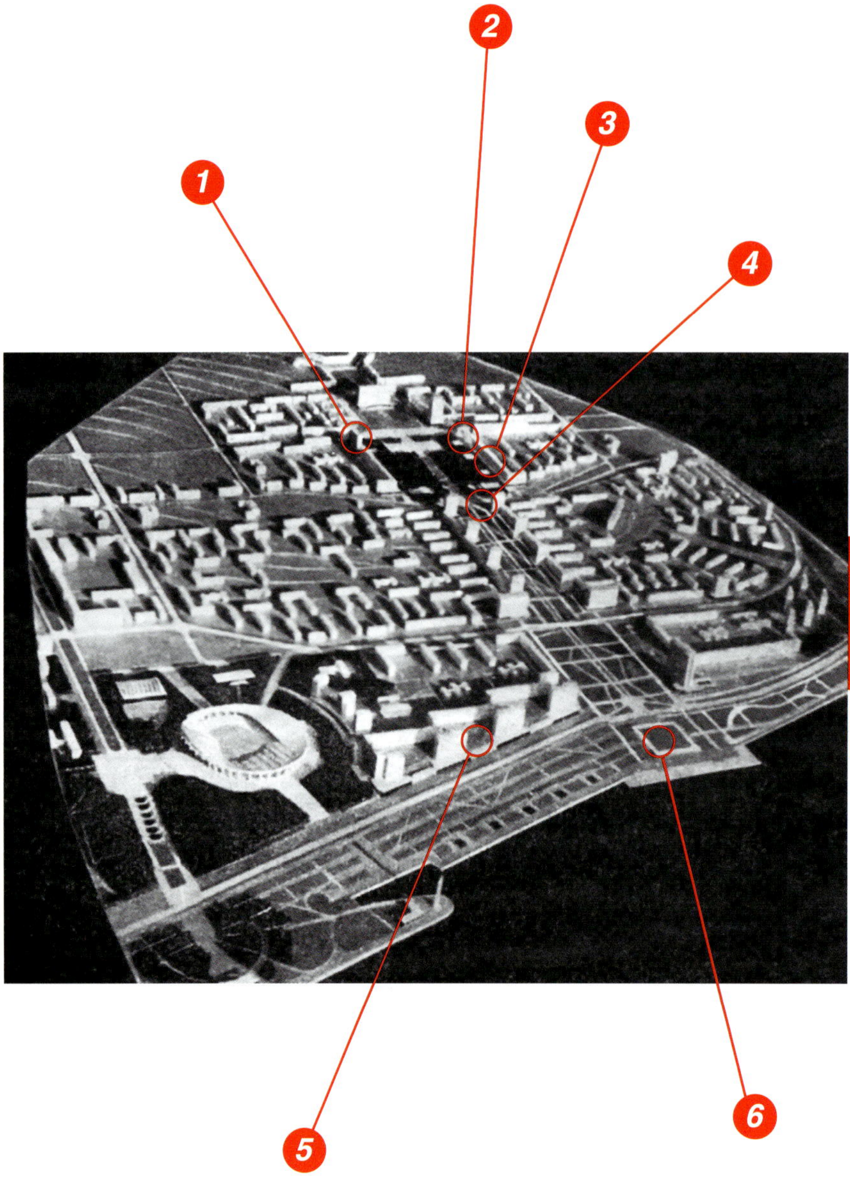

Proposal for the central part of Zaporizhzhia by architects S. Tulchynskyi and N. Kovtun

Hotel on Central Boulevard

2

New post office on Central Boulevard.
Monumental mosaic: Oleksii Konopelko, 1967

3

Residential building
on Central Boulevard

Central Blvd.: revision of the classical principles of the urban-planning ensemble

4

Central Boulevard between micro-districts Nos. 100–101 and 113–115. Perspective view

5

Part of the development of the embankment
with high-rise buildings. Perspective view

Central Blvd.: revision of the classical principles of the urban-planning ensemble

'The architecture of the high-rise residential buildings that form the development front is simple and concise. Its large scale is commensurate with the wide expanses of water. The use of the technique of contrasting elongated residential buildings with tower blocks and large, open, architecturally organised spaces is successful. Construction of 9- and 14-storey residential buildings is planned along Central Boulevard. In the upper part of the boulevard the development organically merges into the space of

the Festival Square. Hotel buildings play a special role. One creates an emphasis at the beginning of the Central Boulevard; the other, on the embankment.'

From 'Construction of the centre of Zaporizhzhia', an article by architects S. Tulchynskyi and N. Kovtun (Construction and Architecture, 1967, No. 7)

6

Panoramic view of Zaporizhzhia from the Dnipro River

Heroiiv (Zhovtneva) Square, 2012. Photo: D. Novikov, 2012

Central Blvd.: revision of the classical principles of the urban-planning ensemble

Models of high-rise buildings on Central Boulevard, Archive of the Zaporizhzhia Regional Organisation of the National Union of Architects of Ukraine

Eastern front of the Festyvalna Square development, seen from the main avenue, 1987, photo by V. Khmara

Western front of the Festyvalna Square development, seen from the main avenue, 1987, photo by V. Khmara

Festyvalna Square. Photo: D. Novikov, 2012

Layout of the development of the waterfront in the central planning area. Archive of Zaporizhzhia Regional Organisation of the National Union of Architects of Ukraine

Central Blvd.: revision of the classical principles of the urban-planning ensemble

Sketch proposal for spatial design of the intersection of the Central Boulevard and the embankment. S. Prudkyi, second half of the 1980s

The systematic development of Pushkin (Vernadskyi) Square began in 1959 after construction of the highway across the dam connecting the old part of the city with the Central District (Voznesenka). In March 1960 S. Vasylevskyi, the city's chief architect, described the then state of affairs as follows: 'Now a printing house and a residential building are being built there. This year, construction of the regional design organisation building is underway – opposite the printing house. To this end, we shall remove some of the old houses adjacent to the building of the regional consumers' society. The city will thus begin to take on a more pleasant appearance than it currently has. In the next few years a school and a number of residential buildings will be built, as well as commercial and culinary schools. The tram line will stay where it is; the buildings will face it like this [he demonstrates]. On this side of the avenue, construction is being carried out a little differently, and the future route goes off more or less along the bisector. Here there'll be a printing house and a design organisation building of the same size. They make for a smart entry to the old part of the city.' One of the most distinctive features of the Pushkin Square ensemble is the proximity of residential buildings of contrasting volumes along the main thoroughfare. The elongated six-storey building (containing the Children's World store) was built in 1966, and the twelve-storey building (housing Kobzar Bookshop) was erected in 1969. A significant event in the further development of Pushkin Square as a Modernist urban-planning ensemble was the construction of the design organisations building (subsequently: the Zaporizhzhia branch of Ukrmiskbudproject); naturally, this provoked heightened interest in the architectural design proposals. In contrast to the large urban formations of the previous, Neoclassical, era, the new Modernist ensemble depended for its compositional unity on the degree to which the observer was involved in the high-speed movement of the main avenue. The ensemble's dual-core composition acquired its final form in the early 1970s with the completion of the Yuvileinyi consumer-services complex with a palace for ceremonial events and a residential building with Lakhti Restaurant on its ground floor in 1973.

Pushkin Square: a composition intended to be seen in dynamic movement

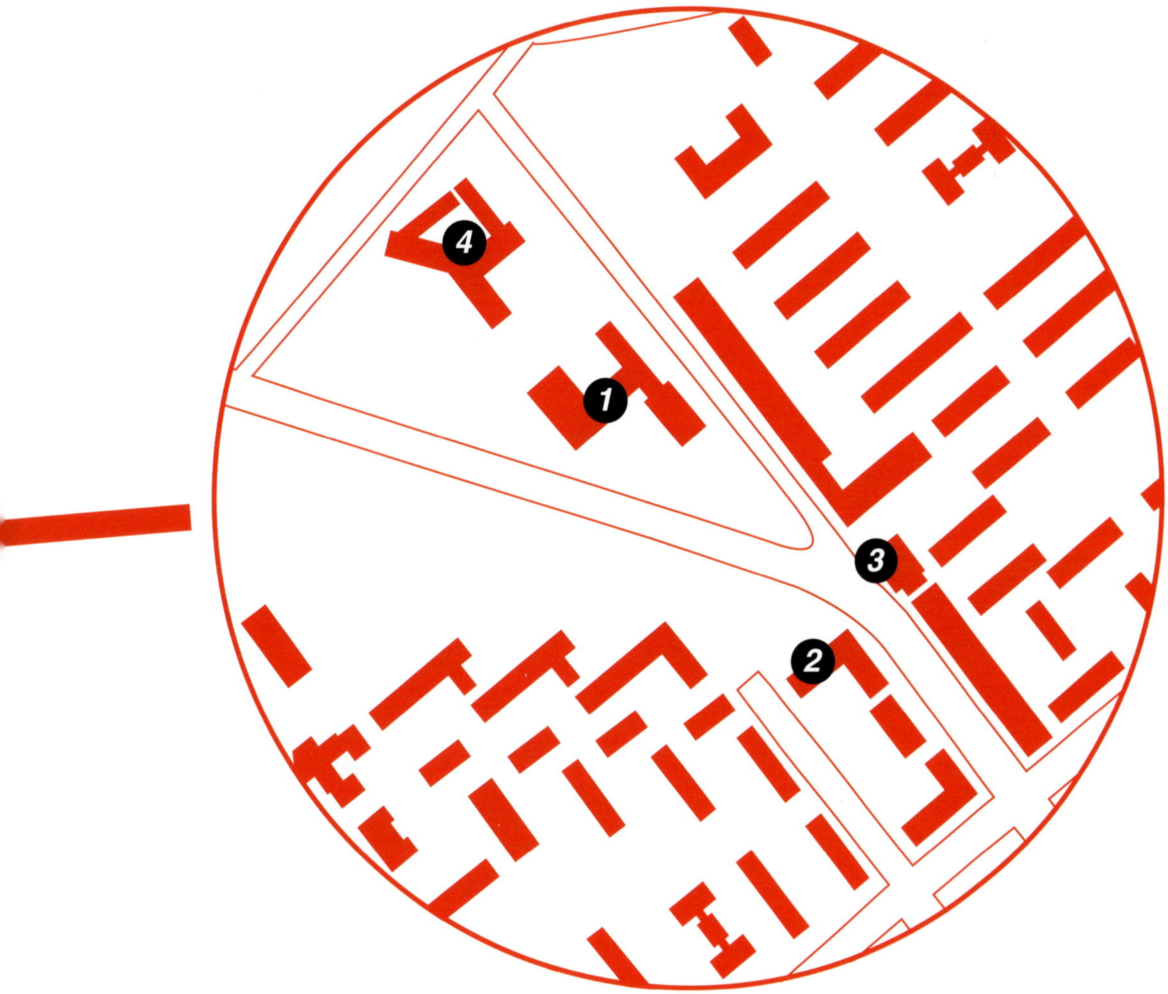

Diagram showing the layout of Pushkin Square and surrounding areas

Yuvileinyi consumer-services centre with the palace for ceremonial events on Vernadskyi Square

Pushkin Square: a composition intended to be seen in dynamic movement

ЗГП

Pushkin Square: a composition intended to be seen in dynamic movement

The complex of Zaporizhtsyvilproject Design Institute, from the book Architecture of Ukraine at the present stage, 1984

Perspective view of the Vernadskyi Square ensemble from the north west

TO KOBZAR!

Like that freedom which has passed

the Dnipro is wide as the sea,

steppe and steppe, roaring rapids,

and graves – like mountains_

there was born and frolicked

the Cossack freedom.

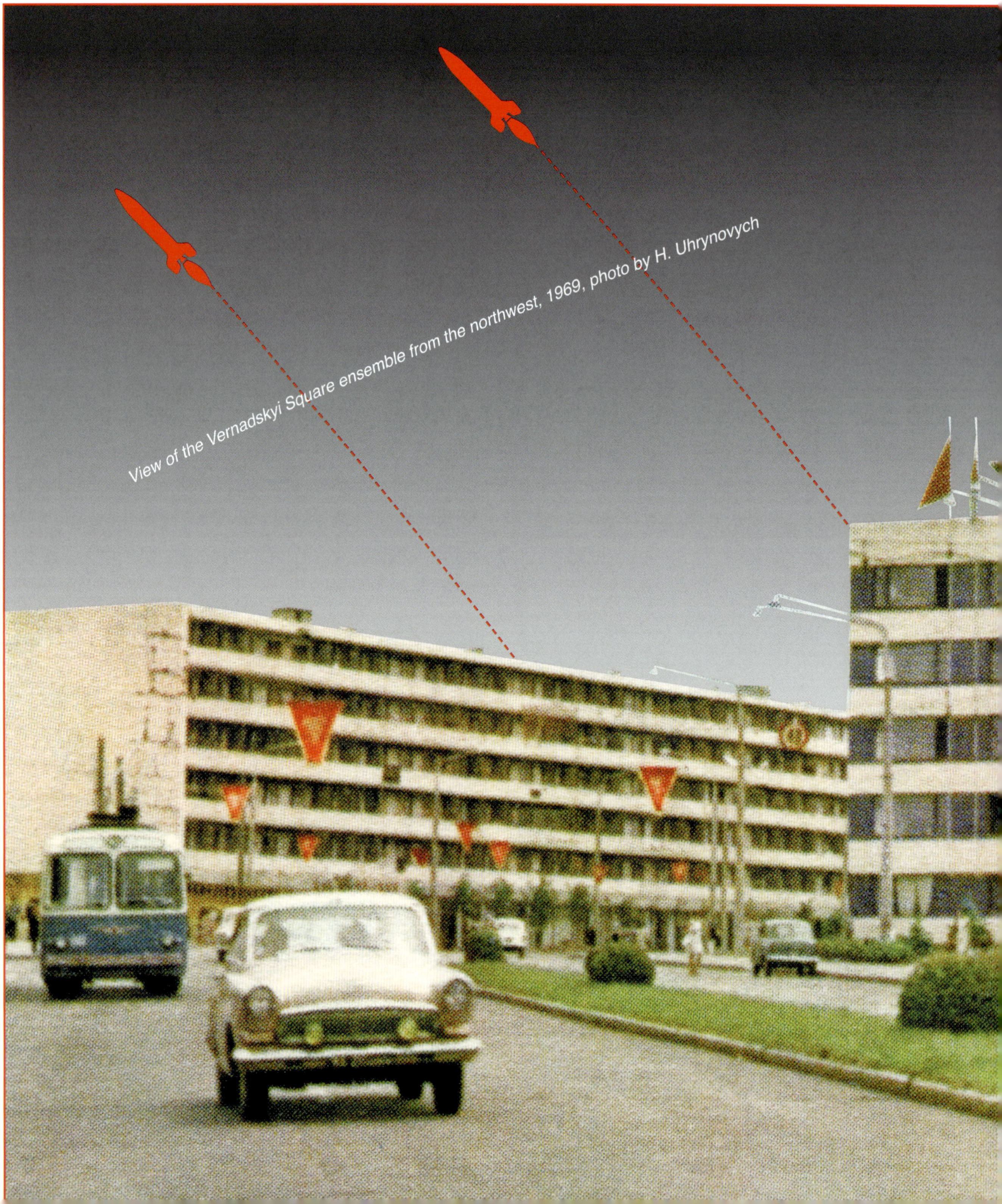

View of the Vernadskyi Square ensemble from the northwest, 1969, photo by H. Uhrynovych

Pushkin Square: a composition intended to be seen in dynamic movement

Perspective view of the Vernadskyi Square ensemble from the southeast. Archive of Zaporizhzhia Regional Organisation of the National Union of Architects of Ukraine

Design proposal for the south-eastern part of the Pushkin Square ensemble. Archive of the Zaporizhzhia Regional Organisation of the National Union of Architects of Ukraine

Lakhti Restaurant

Pushkin Square: a composition intended to be seen in dynamic movement

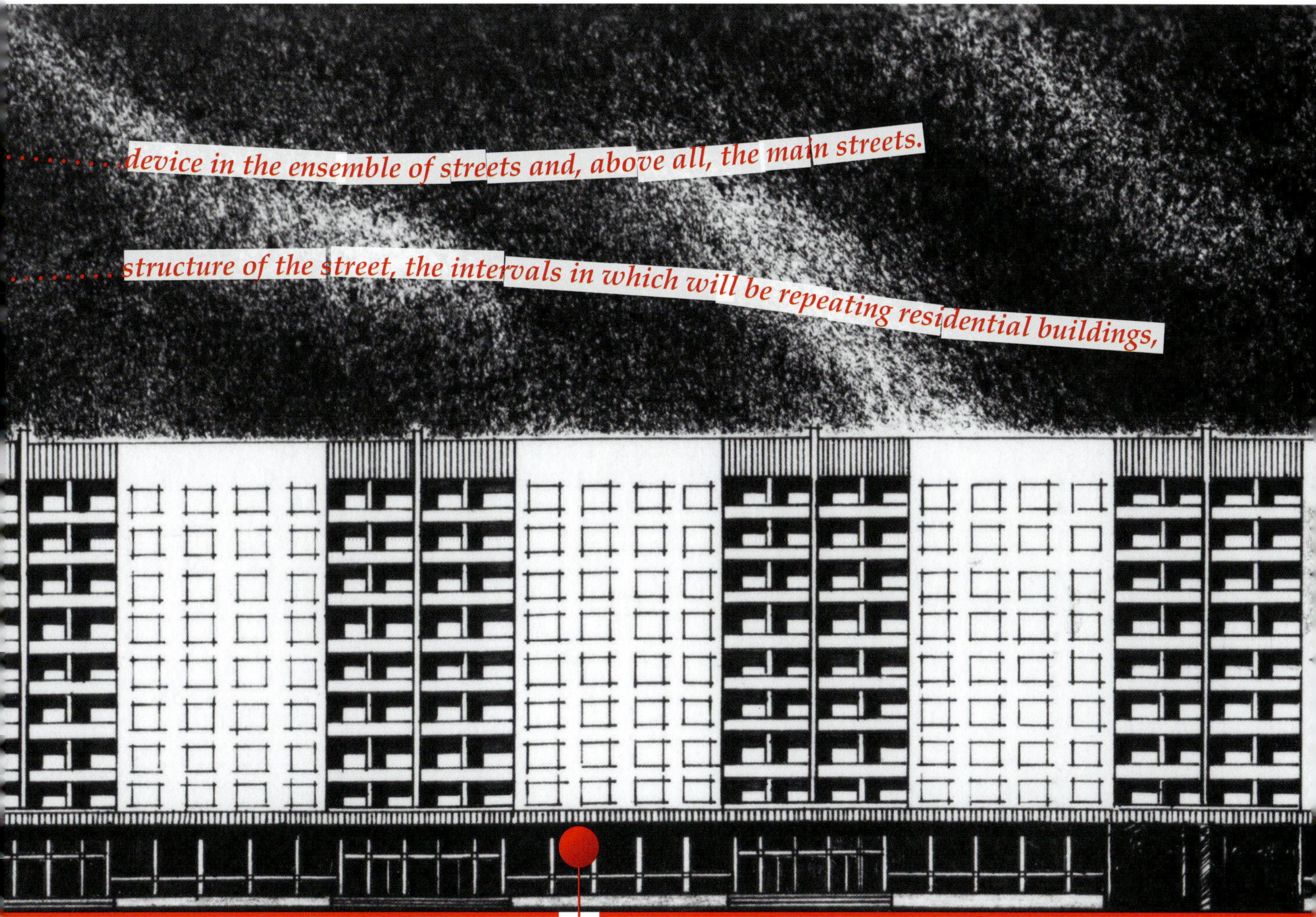

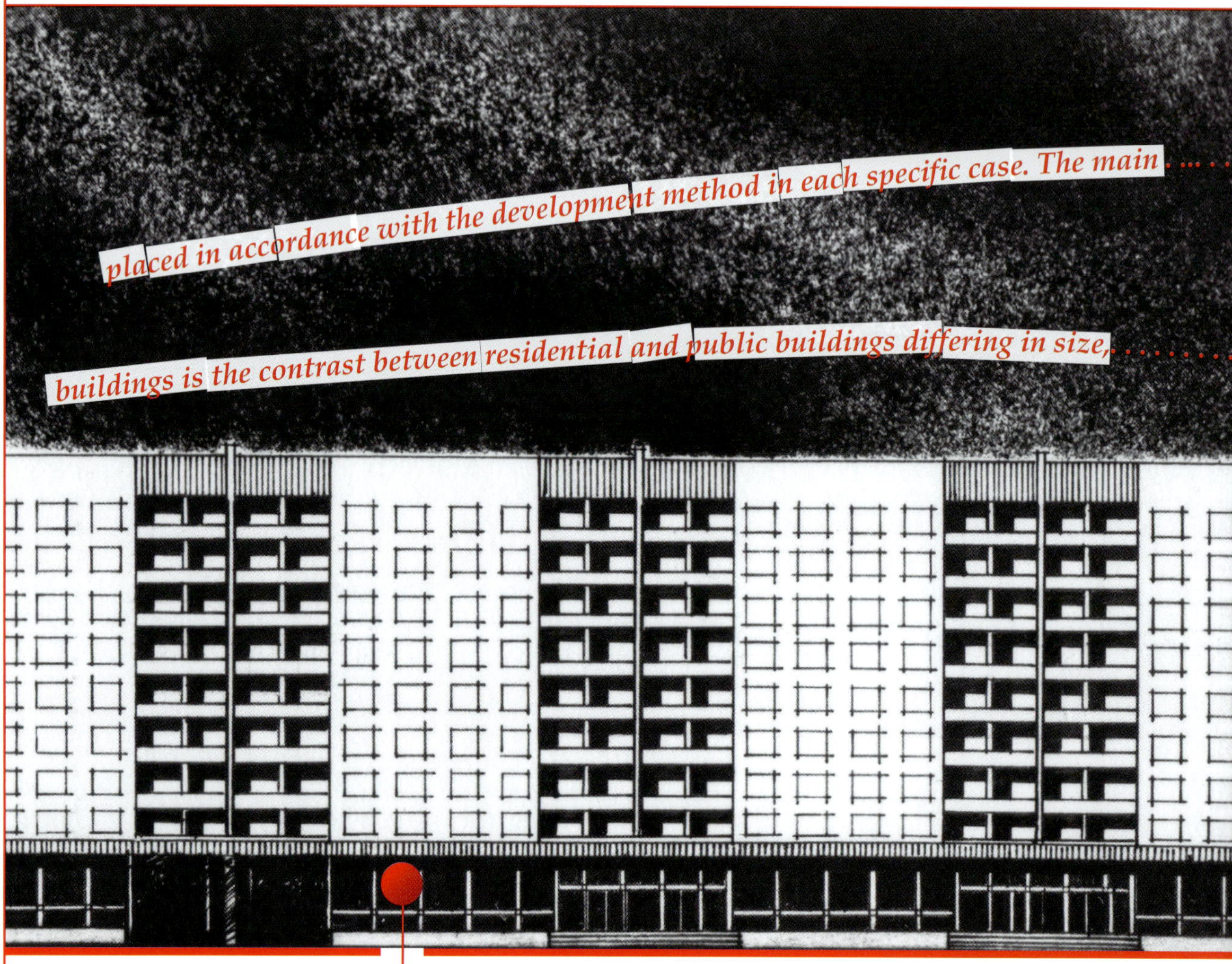
placed in accordance with the development method in each specific case. The main
buildings is the contrast between residential and public buildings differing in size,

Food shop

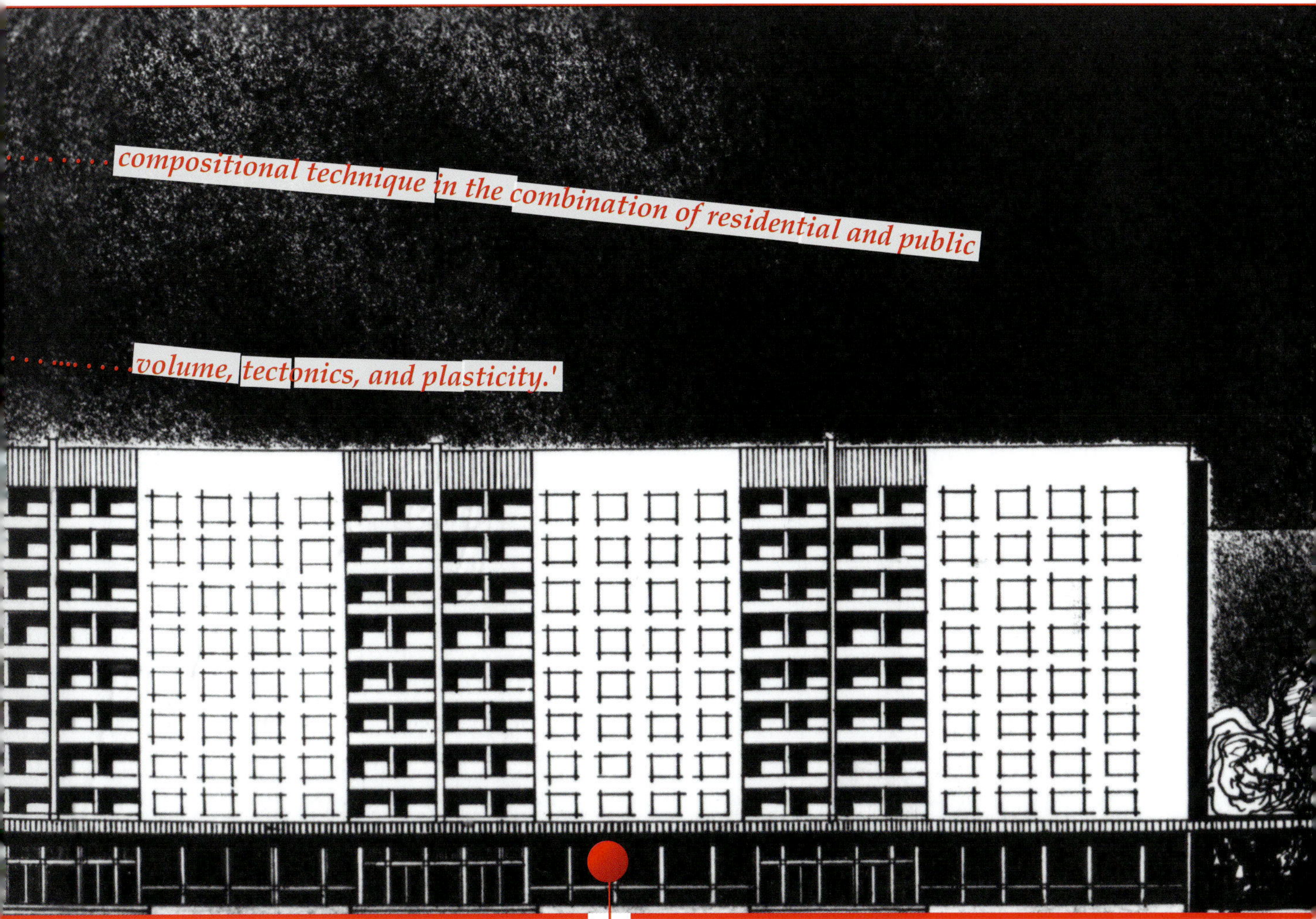

Post office and communications office

On the expressiveness of Modernist ensembles, from a collective monograph published by the Research Institute for Theory, History, and Prospective Problems in Soviet Architecture at the Ukrainian SSR State Construction Department

Commercial and information centre

Pushkin Square: a composition intended to be seen in dynamic movement

Regional universal science library

Creators of modern Zaporizhzhia

208
209

Zaporizhzhia never developed an architectural school of its own. However, it is easy to name a pleiad of professionals whose creativity gives us reason to speak of a Zaporizhzhian approach to architectural education. Local traditions arose where the influences of the powerful Kharkiv and Kyiv design centres intersected. In 1978 the experience gained in interaction with these influences was organisationally embodied in Zaporizhtsyvilproject Design Institute.

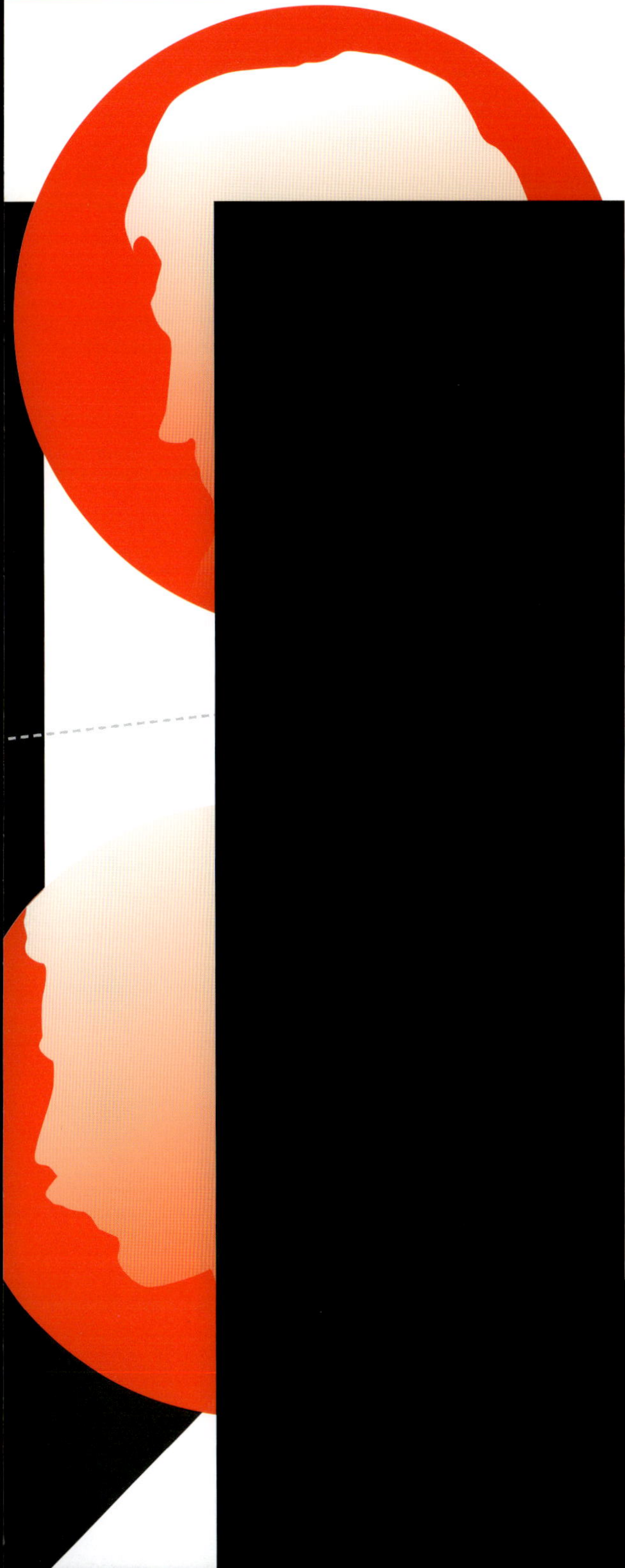

The founding of this institute was a recognition at republican level of the professional skills of architects from Zaporizhzhia. This mainly related to the so-called 'generation of mentors', which included, Mykola Zharikov, Oleksandr Nemonov, Leontii Zaitsev, and Natan Sviet.

Fundamental training by experienced architects and inspiration from the scale of transformation going on around them explain the eagerness with which new generations of architects set about forming a modern urban environment in the 1960s–1980s. Each of the participants in this creative fiesta deserves a separate study. But let's start with the professional achievements of the masters who directly impacted how 'micro-district' residential areas were built in Zaporizhzhia.

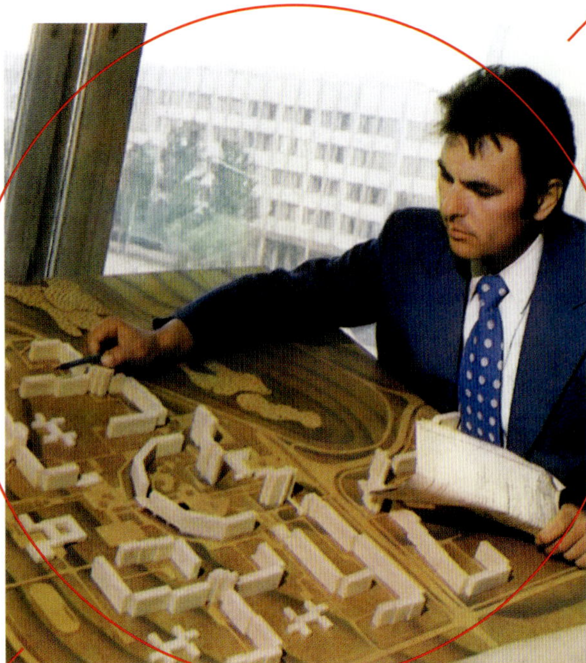

Yurii Biriukov, architect, author of development projects (member of creative team), chief architect for the project for development of micro-districts in the Shevchenkivskyi and Khortytskyi residential areas. Graduated from Kyiv Engineering and Construction Institute in 1965. Worked at the Zaporizhzhia branch of Ukrmiskbudproject (1965–1978). Was the first director of Zaporizhtsyvilproject Design Institute (1978–1982). Was chief architect of Zaporizhzhia Region (1982–2002).

YURII BIRIUK

Adaptation of a standard circus building project (together with Serhii Shestopal). The original project was by the Central Scientific Research Institute for Standardised and Experimental Design of Entertainment Buildings (architects: M. Shulmeister, Yu. Motorin, O. Kudriavtsev).

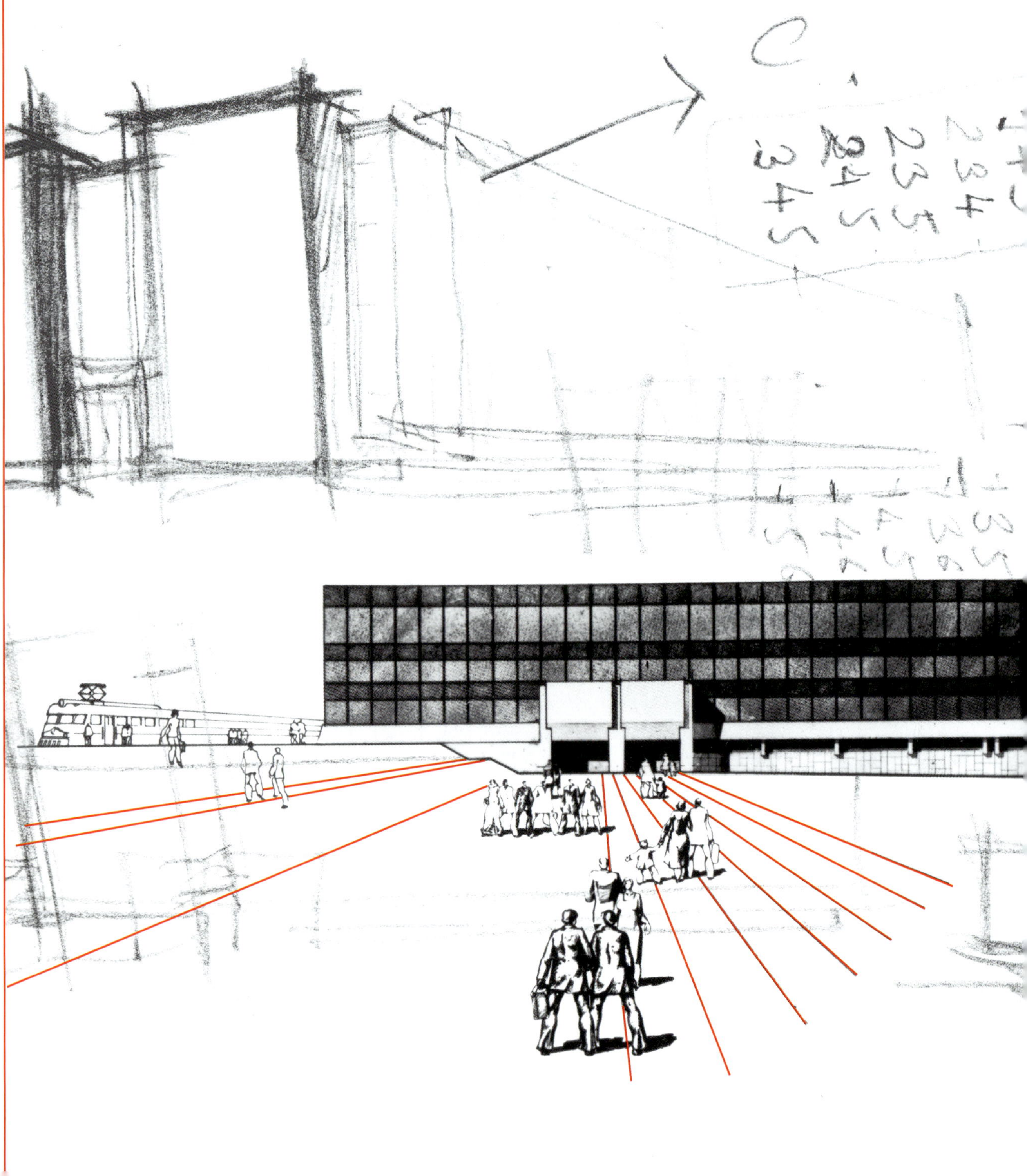

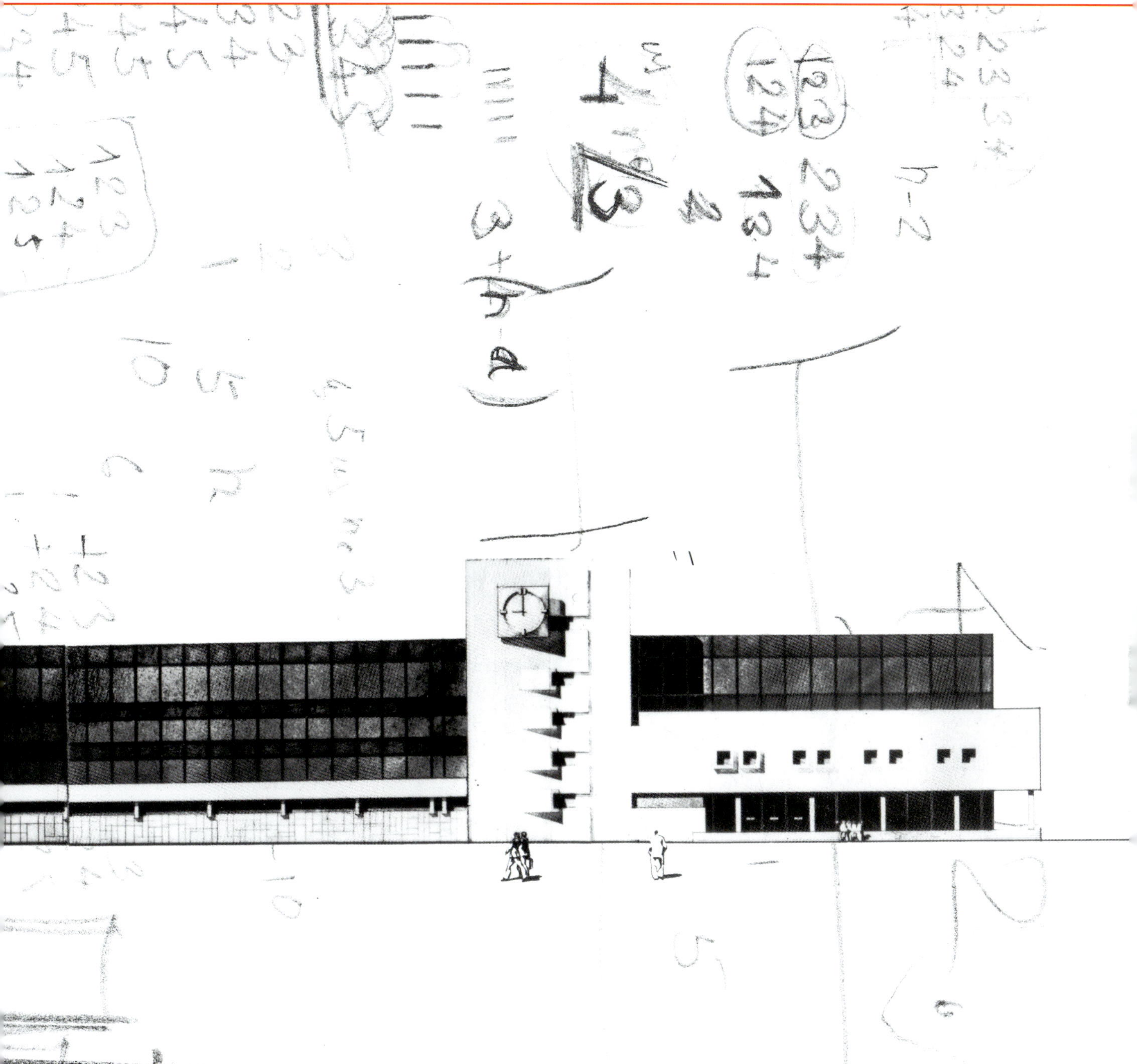

Principal sorting post office near railway station, 1977

Tetiana Shchehlova, architect, lead designer (member of creative team), principal architect for the project for micro-district development in the Pivdennyi residential area ('Pisky'). Graduated from Zaporizhzhia Construction Technical College in 1966. From 1966 to 1968: worked at the design bureau of Zaporizhzalizobeton. From 1968 to 1970: worked at the Zaporizhzhia branch of Ukrmiskbudproject. From 1970 to 1976: studied at Kharkiv Engineering and Construction Institute. In 1976: continued her work at the Zaporizhzhia branch of Ukrmiskbudproject. Since 1978 her career has been closely associated with Zaporizhtsyvilproject Design Institute.

TETIANA SHCHE

HLOVA

Architectural design for the mass-events hall at Zhovtnevyi ('Dniprospetsstal') Palace of Culture, as part of a creative team

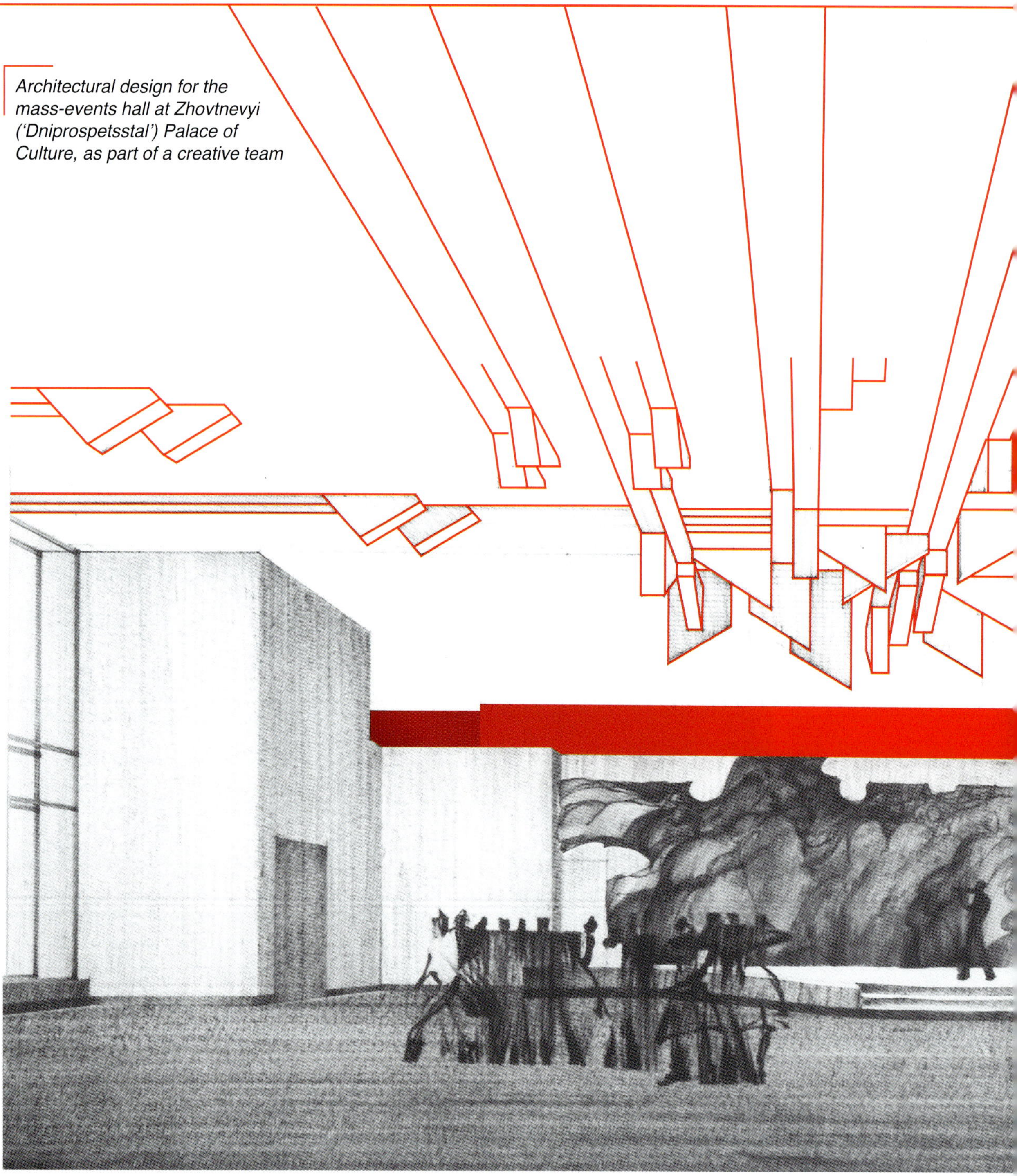

Tetiana Shchehlova

Restoration project for Balabukh Manor on the corner of Petro Sahaidachnyi and Andriivska streets in Kyiv, co-author

Tetiana Shchehlova

Layouts for the Pivdennyi residential area in Zaporizhzhia

Svitlana Fomina, architect, lead project designer (member of creative team), principal architect of the project for micro-district development in the Shevchenkivskyi residential area. Graduated from Kharkiv Engineering and Construction Institute in 1972, the year in which she also started working at the Zaporizhzhia branch of Ukrmiskbudproject (Zaporizhtsyvilproject from 1978 forwards). In 1992 she was one of the first Ukrainian architects to establish her own private architecture firm, Architectural Workshop of S. Fomina, where she worked until 2012.

SVITLANA FOMINA

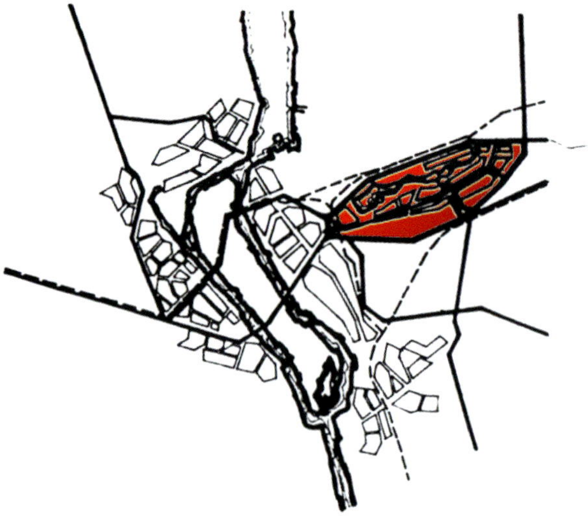

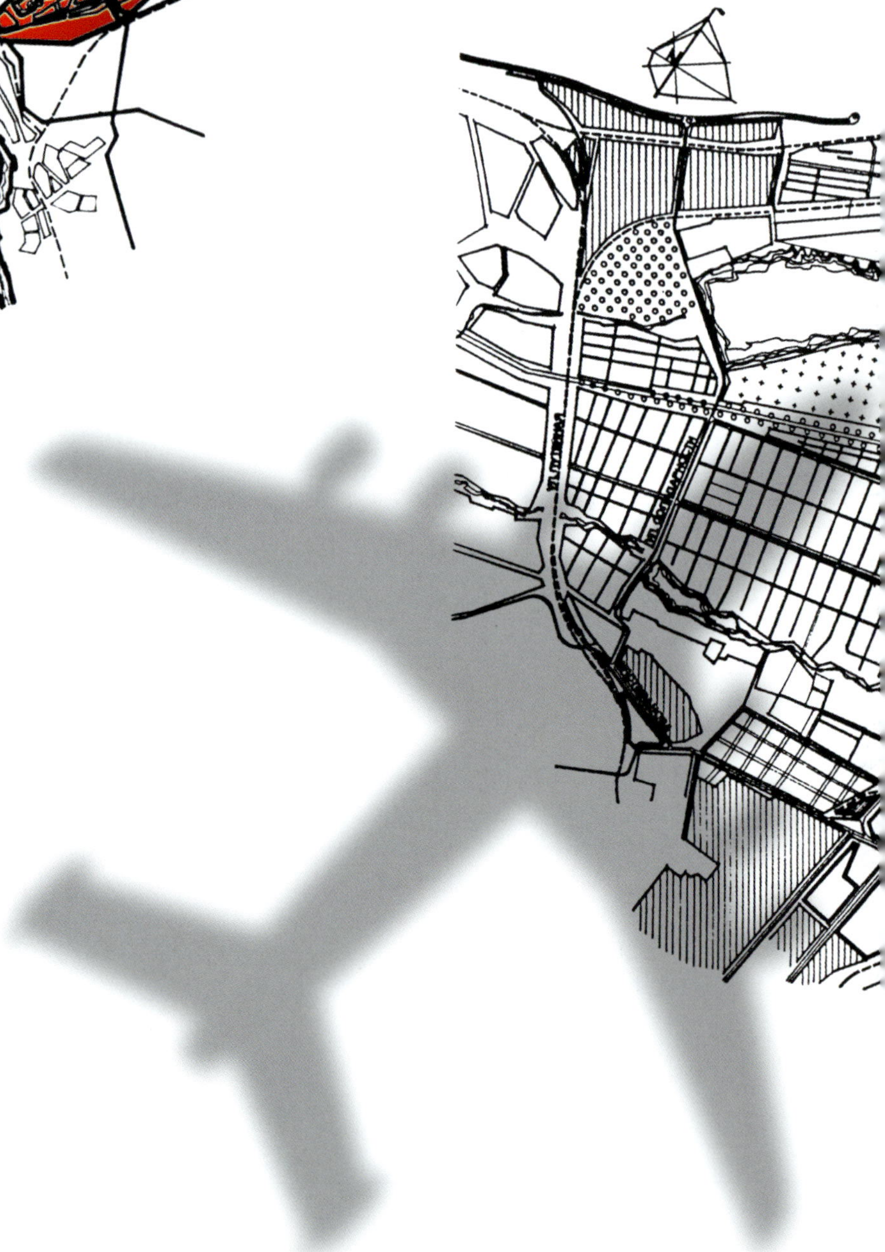

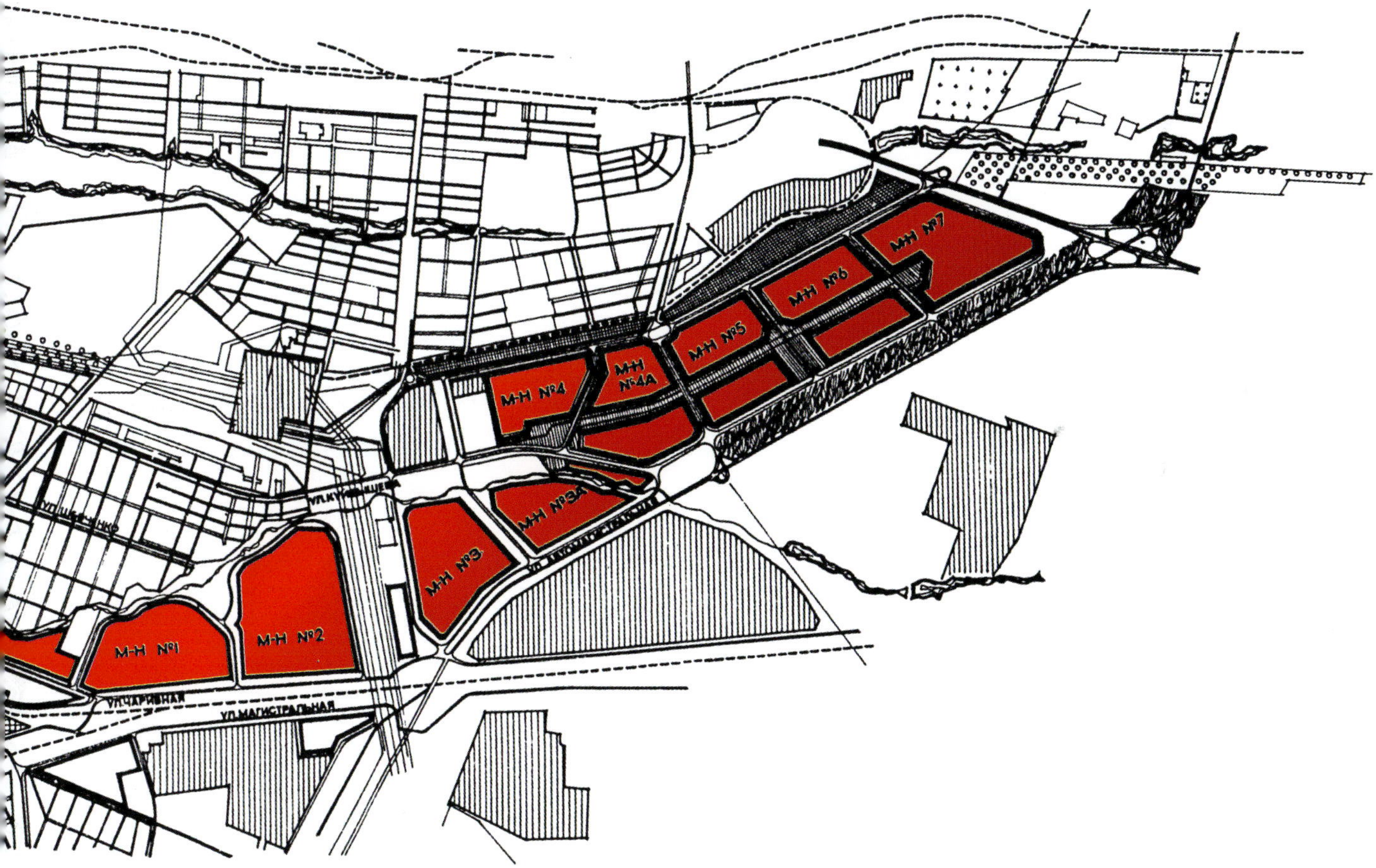

Development project for the Shevchenkivskyi planning area, 1989

Development project for micro-district on Zelenodolska Street in the Shevchenkivskyi residential area (design lead on the project)

Residential buildings 2, 3, 4. Facade on Morobudivnykiv Ave.

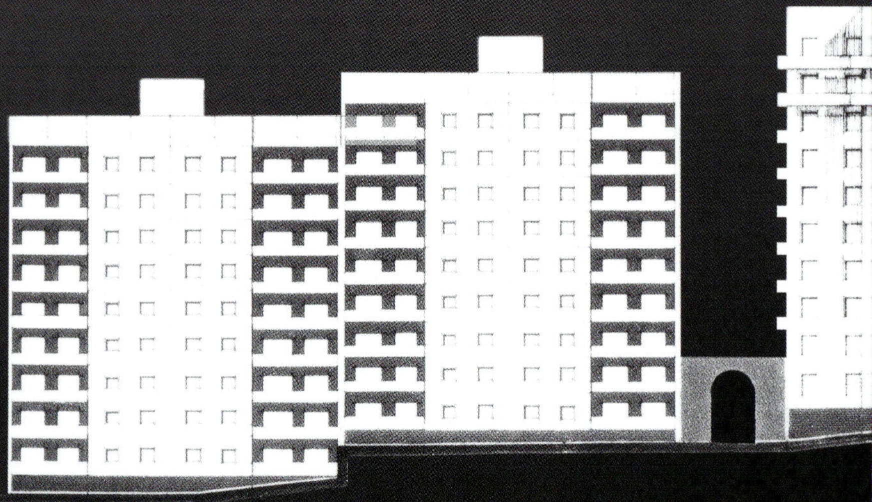

Residential buildings 2, 3, 4. Facade on Charivna Street

230
231

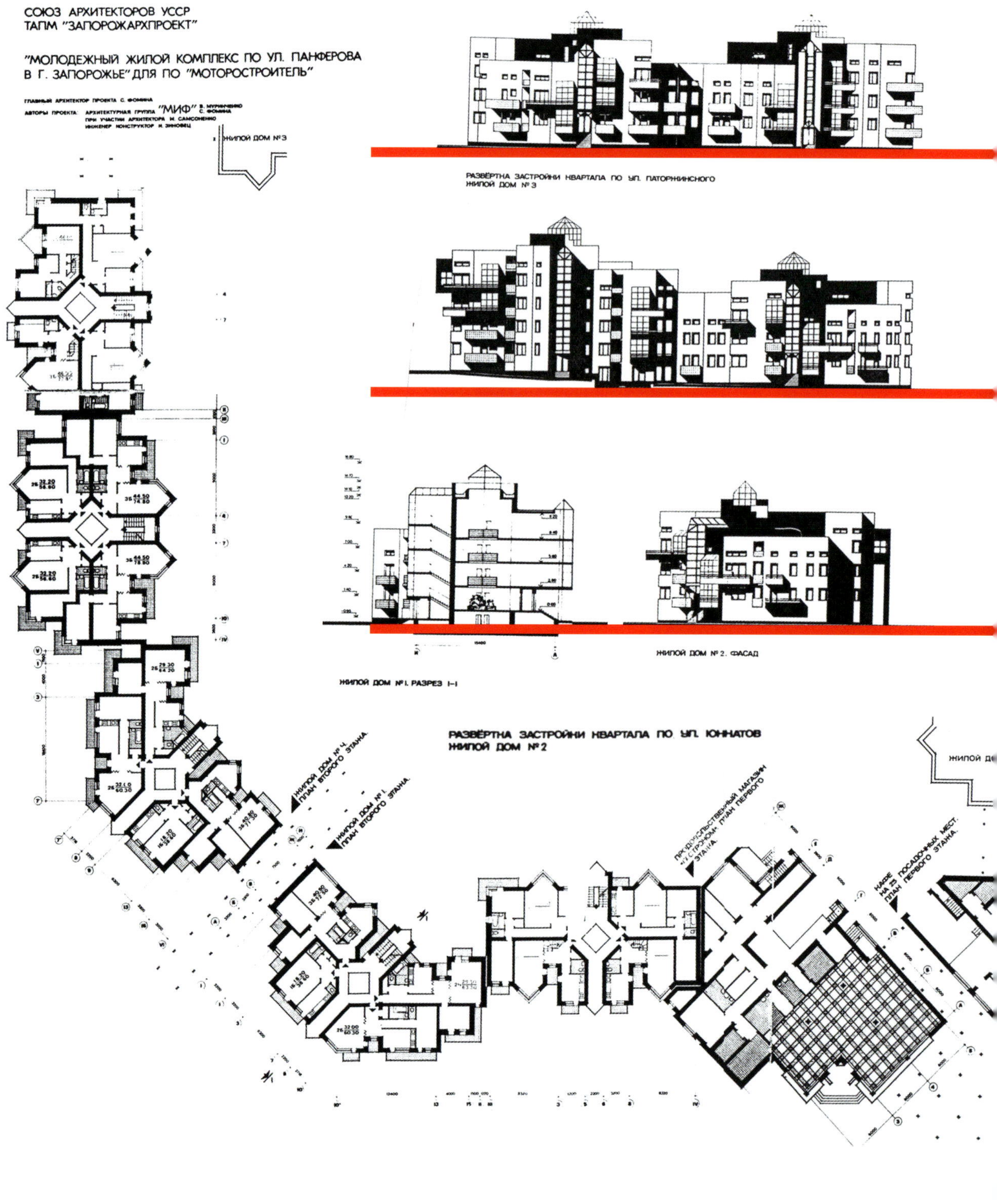
СОЮЗ АРХИТЕКТОРОВ УССР
ТАПМ "ЗАПОРОЖАРХПРОЕКТ"
"МОЛОДЕЖНЫЙ ЖИЛОЙ КОМПЛЕКС ПО УЛ. ПАНФЕРОВА
В Г. ЗАПОРОЖЬЕ" ДЛЯ ПО "МОТОРОСТРОИТЕЛЬ"
ГЛАВНЫЙ АРХИТЕКТОР ПРОЕКТА С. ФОМИНА
АВТОРЫ ПРОЕКТА: АРХИТЕКТУРНАЯ ГРУППА "МИФ" В. МУРИНЧЕНКО С. ФОМИНА
ПРИ УЧАСТИИ АРХИТЕКТОРА И. САМСОНЕНКО
ИНЖЕНЕР КОНСТРУКТОР И. ЗИНОВЕЦ
ЖИЛОЙ ДОМ №3
РАЗВЁРТКА ЗАСТРОЙКИ КВАРТАЛА ПО УЛ. ПАТОРЖИНСКОГО
ЖИЛОЙ ДОМ №3
ЖИЛОЙ ДОМ №1. РАЗРЕЗ 1-1
ЖИЛОЙ ДОМ №2. ФАСАД
РАЗВЁРТКА ЗАСТРОЙКИ КВАРТАЛА ПО УЛ. ЮННАТОВ
ЖИЛОЙ ДОМ №2

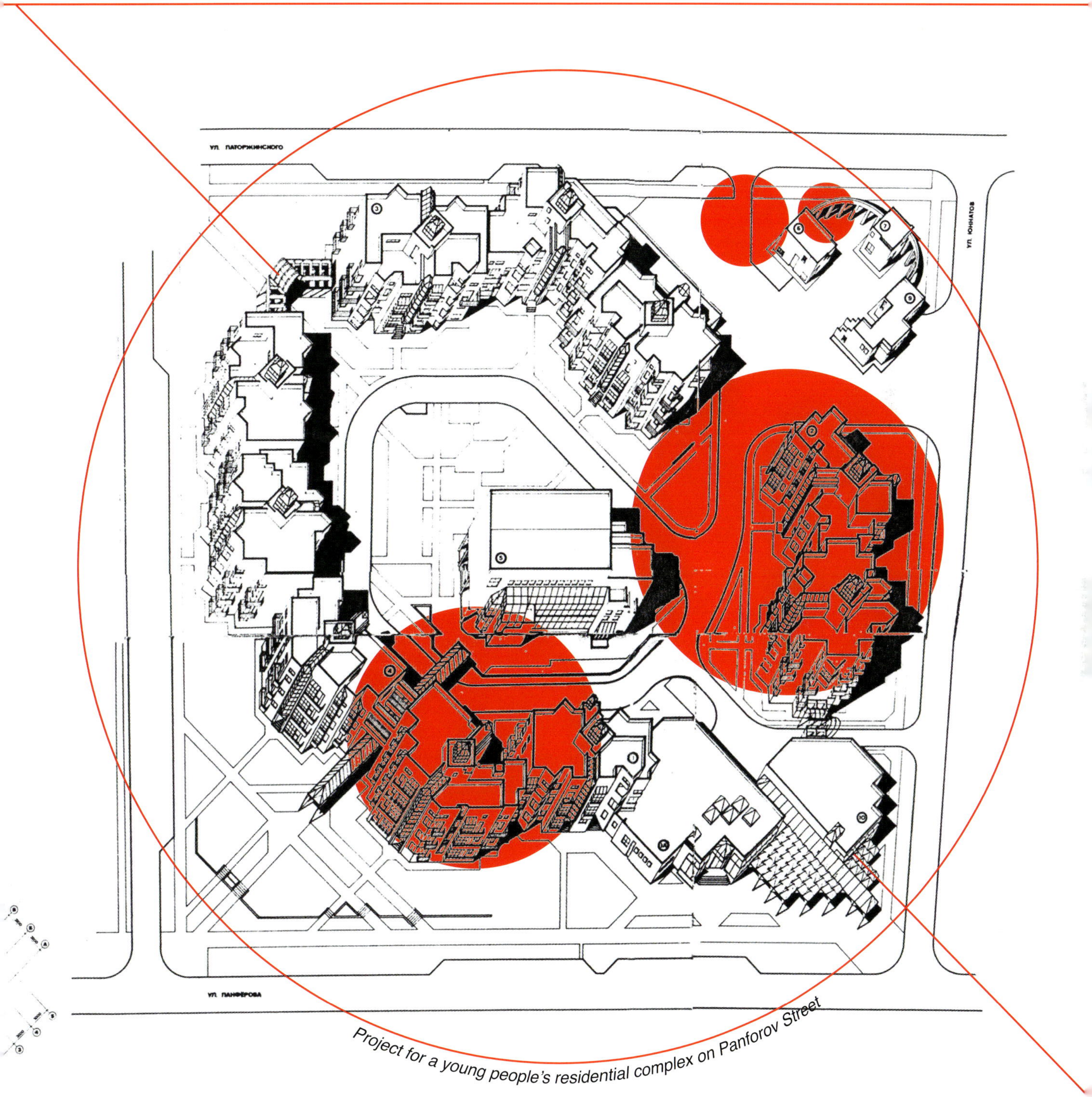

Project for a young people's residential complex on Panforov Street

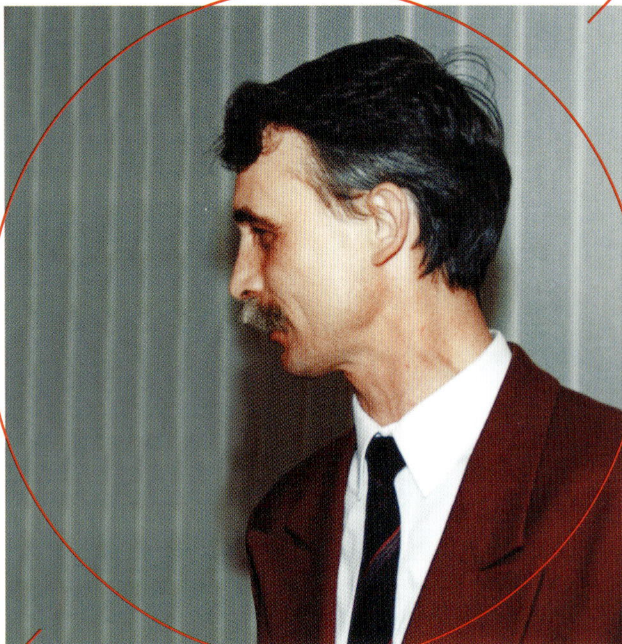

Serhii Prudkyi, architect, one of the authors (as part of a creative team) of the micro-district development of the Osypenkivskyi residential area. Graduated from Dnipropetrovsk Engineering and Construction Institute in 1975. From 1975 to 1996: worked at Zaporizhtsyvilproject Design Institute. From 1996 to 2000: chief architect of the city of Zaporizhzhia. From 2000 to 2006: private architectural practice. From 2006 to 2007: chief architect of Zaporizhzhia Region.

SERHII PRUDK

YI

TV studio complex on Matrosov Street

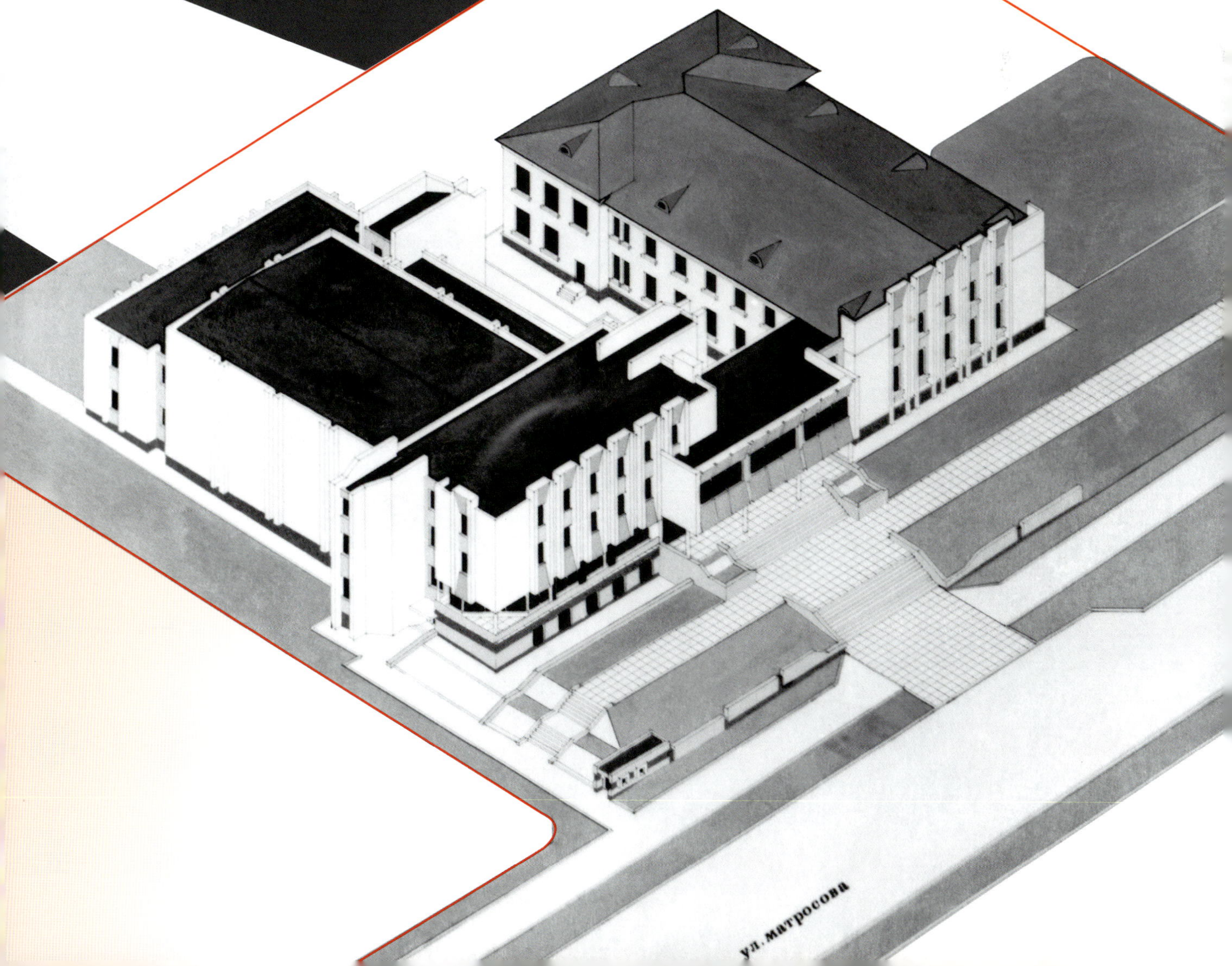
ул. матросова

Building with a variable number of floors on Tahanska Street, massing model.

PET

Vadim Petrenko, architect, lead project designer (part of a creative team) for the micro-district development of the Borodinskyi residential area. Graduated from Kyiv Engineering and Construction Institute in 1980. Worked at Zaporizhtsyvilproject Design Institute until 1992 and from 1996 to 2007. From 1992 to 1996: chief architect at Interproiekt. Since 2007: chief architect and co-founder of AS-Project LLC.

VADIM

RENKO

Massing model for a residential and office complex at the intersection of Gagarin Street and Sobornyi Avenue

Vadim Petrenko

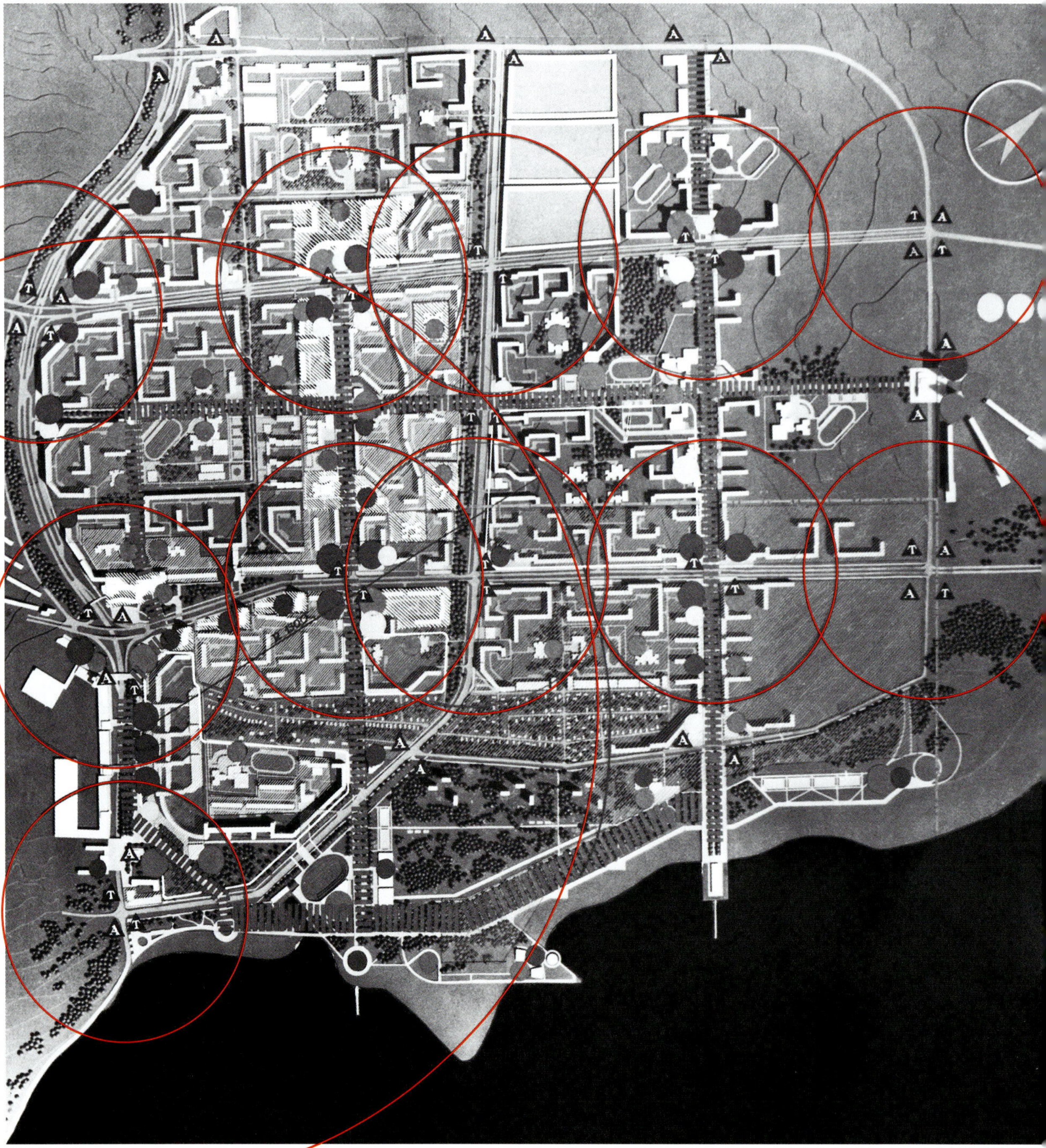

Vadim Petrenko

Development project for Borodinskyi residential area, Zaporizhtsyvilproject, 1985

ECO Tower business centre on Sobornyi Avenue in Zaporizhzhia

Vadim Petrenko

Serhii Didenko, architect, one of the authors (member of a creative team) of the (Bombay) micro-district development on Kremlivska Street. Graduated from Kyiv Engineering and Construction Institute in 1984. In the same year started working at Zaporizhtsyvilproject, where he remained until this institute ceased developing design projects in 2018.

SERHII DENKO

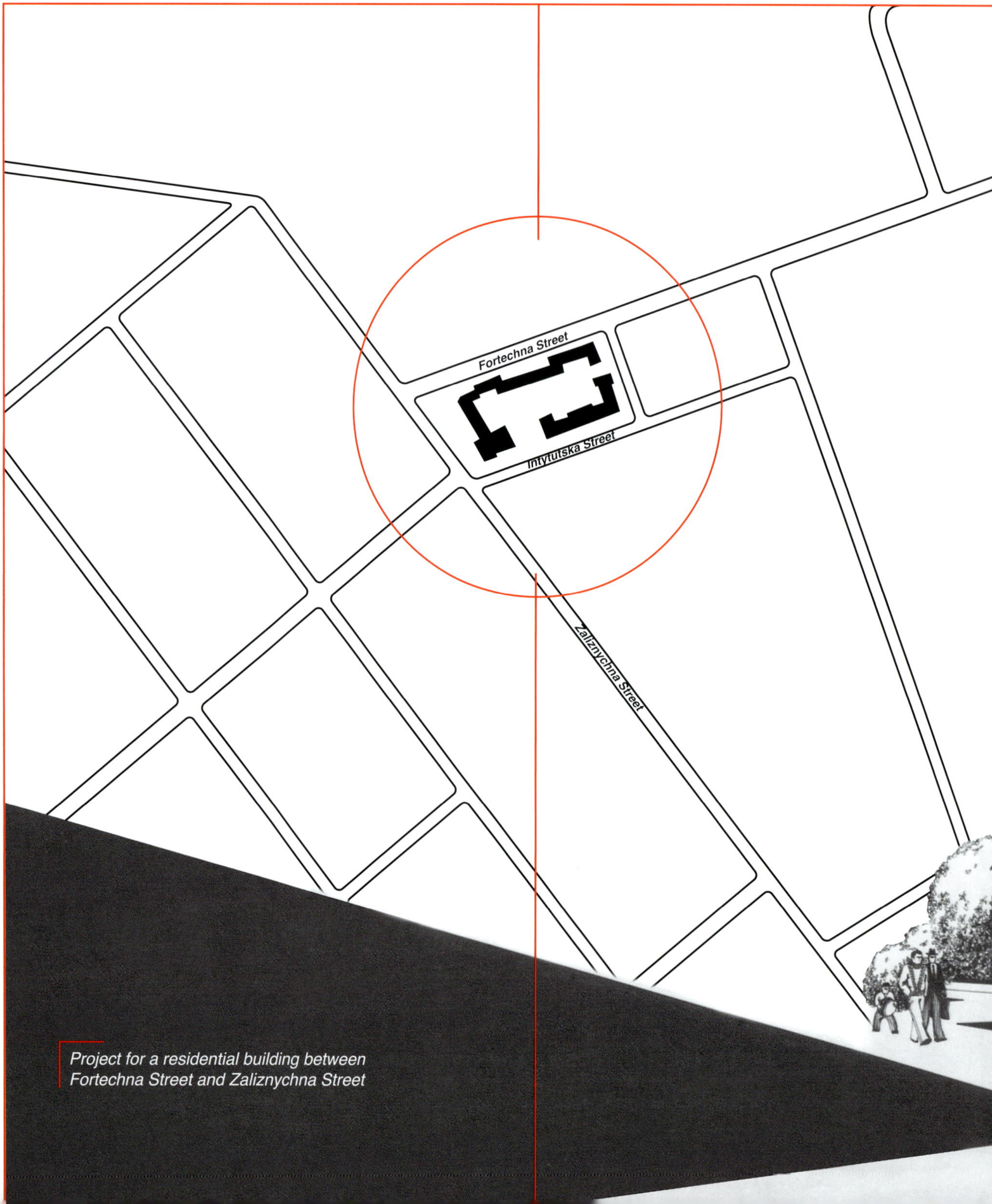

Project for a residential building between Fortechna Street and Zaliznychna Street

Project for a commercial and information centre, Sobornyi Avenue, at Malyi Rynok public-transport stop

HOLOS

Yevhen Holoshchapov, architect, one of the authors (member of the design team) of micro-district development in the Shevchenkivskyi and Khortytskyi residential areas. Graduated from Voronezh Engineering and Construction Institute in 1985. From 1985 to 1991 and from 2006 to 2009: worked at Zaporizhtsyvilproject Design Institute. From 1991 to 1996 worked at Interproiekt. From 2009 to 2010: worked at Hrazhdanproiekt LLC. Since 2010: ECOMM 08 LLC.

YEVHEN
-HCHAPOV

ЖИЛОЙ КОМПЛ
НИАПИ ИНТЕРПРОЕКТ

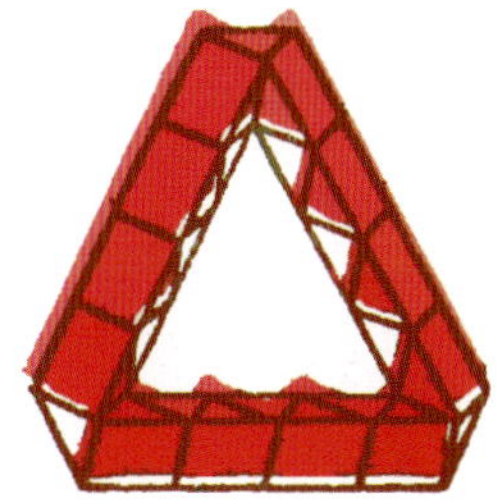

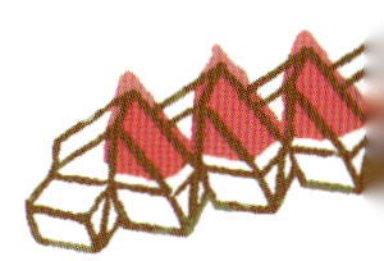

Urban-planning solution for the Skelnyi residential complex (contribution as member of the design team)

CHRONOTOPES

In retelling the history of the largest Zaporizhzhia residential areas that are spread out on both banks of the River Dnipro increasingly acquires the character of legend, a story that is surprisingly far from the actual course of events. In order to restore, at least in outline, the temporal and spatial conditions in which the main residential areas took shape, below we give brief historical references for each of them – where possible, indicating the masters of urban planning who took part in their formation.

LEFT BANK

Kosmichnyi residential area

The brief for the development of a detailed planning project for a housing estate in the vicinity of Orikhivske Highway (since 1961: Kosmichna Street / Highway) on the territory of the former DOS-AAF airfield was approved in 1958. In 1959 Dipromisto devised a project involving construction of micro-districts and a separate public and shopping centre. Further project support for the development of the territory was provided by the Zaporizhzhia branch of Ukrmiskbudproject, which modified the project documentation by increasing the number of floors and density of the buildings and improving the transport scheme. The total planned built area was 280 hectares.[1] Real systematic high-rise construction on the territory of micro-district No. 1 (bounded by today's Hovorukha, Mahara, Pivnichnokiltseva, Sytova, and Kosmichna streets) began in 1961.[2] Throughout the 1960s the city's executive committee allocated

1. DAZO, f. P-2961, op. 1, spr. 98
2. DAZO, f. P-75, op. 5, spr. 932

Construction of the Kosmichnyi residential area on the corner of Chumachenko and Yevropeiska streets, 1980s. Photo supplied by Zaporizhzhia Museum of Architecture

RIGHT BANK Khortytskyi residential area

In 1961 Dipromisto produced a project for the planning and development of a residential area in the vicinity of Dniprobud II Station. Oleksandr Rapoport (principal architect of Dipromisto studio No. 5) represented the project from the Republican Institute at local urban-planning bodies. On 10 May 1962 this planning and development project (also known as 'the general plan') was approved by the city's executive committee.[12] As recalled by Rapoport, the Zaporizhzhia architects S. Vasylevskyi, M. Zharikov, P. Ohurtsov, N. Sviat, and S. Shestopal, accompanied by V. Ploshchenko (chairman of the city's executive committee) and M. Kryvobokov, the city's 'smartest man', of the regional department for construction and architecture took an active part in discussion of the project. The city's executive committee began approving the first assignments of plots of land for systematic construction in the late 1960s: micro-districts No. 7,

12. DAZO, f. P-75, op. 5, spr. 994

pp. 34 – 35

Khortytskyi residential area, 1979. Photo by P. Churiukanov, kindly provided by Khortytsia National Reserve

plots for engineering infrastructure and construction of the remaining micro-districts, in particular,
for micro-district No. 2 (17 hectares) in 1961,
for micro-district No. 7 (23 hectares) in 1963,
for micro-district No. 3 (16 hectares) in 1964,
for micro-district No. 6 (26 hectares) in 1965,
for micro-district No. 4 (34 hectares) in 1966,
for micro-district No. 10 (21.3 hectares) in 1967,
for micro-district No. 9 (23 hectares) in 1968.
There is no micro-district number No. 8. A green space (now Gagarin Park) and a public shopping centre were created within the planning boundaries of the site under the provisional number 5. The main client for the construction work was Zaporizhzhia's Capital Construction Department. In some cases this function was assigned to enterprises (both for public and residential construction), namely: enterprise 'mailbox 64' (Radioprylad), the regional consumers' society, Zaporizhenerhobud construction company, Zaporizhzhia House-Building Factory, Zaporizhtsyvilbud production association, Komunar Automobile Factory, the training and production plant for deaf and dumb, the regional production and technical communications office, Zaporizhnerudprom Trust, Zaporizhzhiavodbud construction company, and Ukraine department store. Cooperative construction was carried out by, among other organisations, the Prydniprovsk Railway, the municipal utilities service, the regional production department of motor vehicles, Zaporizhbud construction company (micro-district No. 4, Pivnichnokiltseva, Sytova, and Chumachenko streets), Komunar motor-building plant, Radioprylad, semiconductor plant (micro-district No. 10, Yevropeiska, Olimpiiska, and Chumachenko streets).

pp. 20 – 21

No. 8, and No. 9 in 1968 and micro-district No. 4 in 1969. In 1970, at the initiative of V. Yalanskyi, the deputy chairman of the executive committee, the residential area was given a modern official name: 'The micro-district involving development of Dniprobud-II will henceforth be called "Khortytskyi residential area".'[13] During the 1970s the main design work on systematic construction of the residential area was carried out by the Zaporizhzhia branch of Ukrmiskbudproject. It was at this time that the sectoral initiatives of the State Construction Committee of the Ukrainian SSR strengthened the urban-planning discipline, in particular, through the formation of 'demonstration residential complexes' (Resolution No. 170 of the Council of Ministers of the Ukrainian SSR, dated 6 April 1973). In the Khortytskyi residential area, micro-district No. 6 (now bounded by Svitla Street and Yuvileinyi and Inzhener Preobrazhenskyi avenues) was assigned for the construction of exemplary buildings in 1975–1977. The development of micro-districts No.3 (bounded by Serhiienko, Voronezka, and Heroes of the 93rd Brigade streets) and No. 5 (bounded by Heroes of the 93rd Brigade and Serhiienko streets and Yuvileinyi and Inzhener Preobrazhenskyi avenues) became a much larger 'demon-

13. DAZO, f. P-75, op. 6, spr. 473

pp. 32 – 33

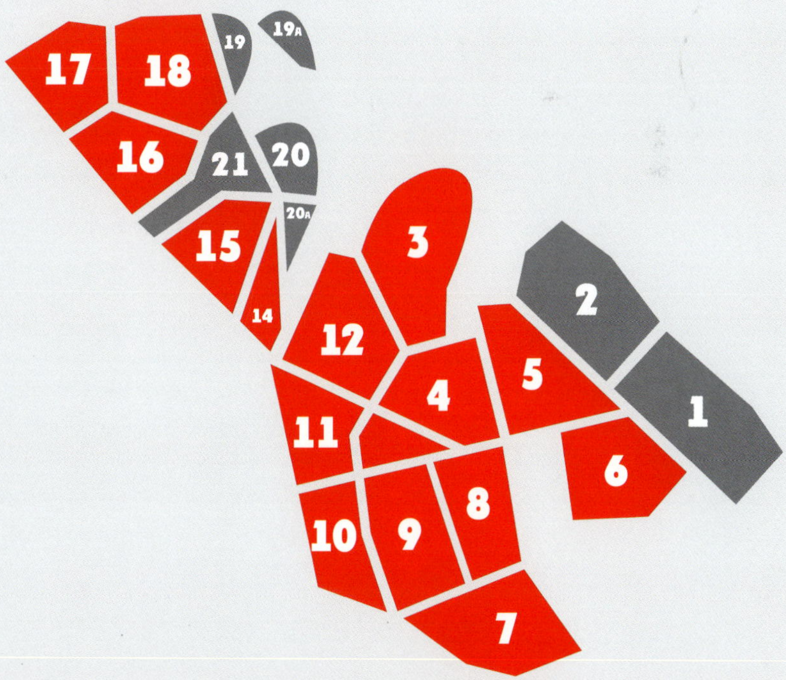

Structure of the micro-district development of the Khortytskyi residential area. Unrealised neighbourhoods are highlighted in grey.

LEFT BANK

Shevchenkivskyi residential area

The detailed planning project for the residential area in Shevchenkivskyi District on the territory of the nursery of the Zelenbud communal enterprise was approved by the technical council of the regional department for construction and architecture on 17 May 1966. The project's developer was the Zaporizhzhia branch of Ukrmiskbudproject. The design team was: S. Shestopal, Yu. Biriukov, and L. Vyshinska.[3] The residential area was built up with two micro-districts consisting of houses of five or more floors built to the standardised designs 1-480A and 1y-438A. The planning brief for the development of micro-district No. 1 (bounded by Tsytrusova, Parkhomenka, Bocharova, and Charivna streets) was examined at the technical council on 2 August 1966. According to the project documentation, the construction cost of one square metre of living space was 139.4 karbovanets. The project for the develop-

3. DAZO, f. P-2654, op. 1, spr. 324

pp. 22 – 23

Development of Shevchenkivskyi micro-district No. 1 on Bocharov Street, 1970. Photo supplied by Zaporizhzhia Museum of Architecture

stration' project. Commenced in 1979, the gruelling struggle to make these micro-districts truly exemplary involved a whole series of measures – above all, the simultaneous commissioning of residential buildings and services infrastructure such as schools and preschool institutions, trade and public-catering enterprises, and household and communal services. Also, in order to preserve the architecture of residential buildings, the city's executive committee instructed 'previously cluttered, blocked-up, or glazed balconies and loggias in all houses, regardless of departmental affiliation, to be cleaned and restored to their condition as originally designed; in the future such phenomena are not to be permitted.'[14] It is worth noting that actual construction in micro-district No. 5 began in 1977, and in micro-district No. 3 in 1978. This means that a number of multi-storey buildings had already been commissioned and their residents were already settling into their new homes when these buildings acquired 'demonstration' status. On this occasion the main construction work was carried out by Zaporizhzhia House-Building Factory and Zaporizhzhytlobud Trust. To organise systematic planning of the work, an automated control system was implemented using the Minsk-32 computer. At the end of the 1970s the planning core of the Khortytskyi residential area had mostly been completed. This consisted of micro-districts Nos. 3–11, a block of educational institutions, and a square between Novhorodska Street and Yuvileinyi Avenue, whose creation had been decided upon by the city's executive committee on 21 March 1974. The square was laid out 'on the site specified in the planning project for the bus station and covered market'.[15]

14. DAZO, f. P- 75, op. 9, spr. 477
15. DAZO, f. P-75, op.6, spr. 965

pp. 36 – 37

ment of micro-district No. 2 (bounded by Bocharova, Parkhomenka, Poliakov, and Charivna streets) was examined on 28 March 1967: 'The architectural and planning approach adopted for micro-district No. 2 is based on building up the city highway connecting the city with the Moscow-Simferopol Highway and on creating links between the interior of the micro-district and a large area of greenery bordering it near the stream and the public centre.'[4] In order to carry out further development of micro-districts, on 21 December 1976 the regional urban-planning council approved the 'detailed planning project for the residential area at the intersection of Charivna Street with the Moscow-Simferopol Highway.' This project's principal architect was L. Vyshynska.[5] To improve transport connections with the new residential area, it was proposed to extend Avramenko Street (then one of the sides of Poliakov Street) to Kuibyshev Street (now Igor Sikorsky Street). Before this, on 27 November 1975, the city's executive committee had assigned a plot of land (46 hectares) for an enlarged urban block as part of the future micro-district development.[6] This urban block was subsequently named 'Shevchenkivskyi micro-district No. 3 (bounded by Avramenko, Igor Sikorsky, Spartak Makovskyi, and Voronin streets)' in the project documentation. Residential buildings were built to standardised designs from Series 480A and Series 87.[7] The first houses on Avramenko (Poliakov) Street were built in 1977. Due to the fact that the next enlarged urban block was included, together with the plot of the first block, inside the limits approved in 1976 for a single micro-district with an area of 76 hectares, in the project documentation it was called 'Shevchenkivskyi micro-district No. 3-a (bounded by Spartak Makovskyi, Igor Sikorsky, and Voronin streets)'. The design brief for the development of micro-district No. 3-a was examined and approved by the regional urban planning council on 25 December 1979. The head of the workshop, O. Yehorov, reported on behalf of Zaporizhtsyvilproject. Use was made of adapted standardised projects of residential buildings from Series 480A and Series 96.[8]

4. DAZO, f. P-2654, op. 1, spr. 354
5. DAZO, f. P-2654, op. 1, spr. 567
6. DAZO, f. P-75, op. 9, spr. 56
7. DAZO, f. P-75, op. 9, spr. 574
8. DAZO, f. P-2654, op. 1, spr. 354

pp. 24 – 25

RIGHT BANK

Borodinskyi residential area

The first stage of development of the Borodinskyi residential area began in 1969: 'Assign to the directorate of the V.I. Lenin Dnipro Hydroelectric Station of the Ministry of Energy and Electrification of the USSR, whose second stage is currently under construction, the 31-hectare plot of land between Murmanska, Ladozhska, May 9, and Aivazovsky streets for the construction of residential buildings. The barracks belonging to the Lenin Dnipro Hydroelectric Station, the prefabricated houses of the leather-goods factory, and the single-family houses along Yaroslavska, May 9, and Enerhetychna streets are to be demolished.'[16] As of 1978, 18 multi-storey buildings, a children's complex with 280 seats, a dining hall with 220 seats, a culinary school, a beer bar, a school for 1176 pupils, grocery and vegetable shops, a post office, a Soiuzpechat branch office, a boiler house, and utility networks had come into operation in micro-dis-

16. DAZO, f. P-75, op. 6, spr. 391

Development of the Borodinskyi residential area, 1980s. Photo supplied by Zaporizhzhia Museum of Architecture

LEFT BANK

Pivdennyi residential area

In the late 1950s and early 1960s the name ‘Pivdennyi residential area’ was used for systematic development in the Kosmichna Street planning area. Since the beginning of the 1980s this name has been officially attached to an integrated micro-district development project on land belonging to Zaporizhzhia Forestry in the vicinity of the Mykolaiv floodplain. On 11 September 1980, on the basis of the technical and economic justification approved by the USSR State Planning Organization on 15 May 1980, the city’s executive committee adopted a decision to allocate a plot of land to Zaporizhzhia’s Capital Construction Department for reclamation of land and subsequent design and construction of micro-districts.[9] On 18 February 1981 the Council of Ministers of the Ukrainian SSR granted permission ‘for construction of the Pivdennyi residential area on a 180-hectare site’ on the land of the state forestry fund.[10] The detailed planning pro-

9. DAZO, f. R -75, op. 9, spr. 542
10. DAZO, f. P-75, op. 9, spr. 633

pp. 222 – 223

Construction of the 1st Pivdennyi micro-district, school for 1568 pupils, 1980s. Photo kindly provided by Zaporizhzhia Museum of Architecture

tricts No. 1 and No. 2 of the Dnipro Hydroelectric Station.[17] In 1981 a start was made on the second stage of housing construction (micro-districts No. 3 and No. 4): 'between Medychna, Zoriana, Zernova, and Panas Myrnyi streets on a 45.5-hectare site with the first phase of construction between Medychna, Zoriana, and Ladozhska streets and the planned boulevard on a 13.5-hectare site.'[18] In all, upon completion of the second stage of construction, 17,120 people were to be additionally accommodated in the residential area. The third stage of development lasted from 1989 to 1994 and for the most part involved the creation of micro-district No. 6, bounded by Medychna, Tovaryska, Marshala Chuikova, and Dniprovski Porohy streets. A distinctive feature of this stage was that the functions of principal client were transferred from Zaporizhzhia's Capital Construction Department to large enterprises such as Dniproenerhoremont, Zaporizhzhia Coke Plant, Zaporizhtransformator, Zaporizhtsyvilbud, and the state cooperative firm Progress.

17. DAZO, f. P-75, op. 9, spr. 395
18. DAZO, f. P-75, op. 9, spr. 637

pp. 42, 242

ject for this residential area with a sketch of three micro-districts in the first stage was developed by Zaporizhtsyvilproject (principal planner: S. Vasyliev) and approved by the city's executive committee on 12 March 1981 with the following comments: 'during the first stage of construction locations are to be assigned for a cinema, a maternity hospital, a clinic, and workshops for the district administration.'[11] Land reclamation in micro-district No. 1 (between Pryberezhna Highway and Sorok Rokiv Peremohy, Vodohraina, and Novokuznetska streets) was completed in 1984. Land reclamation in this residential area continued until the early 1990s, stopping at the site for micro-district No. 7. The boundaries for what was intended to be micro-district No. 8 now contain Kushuhum Lake. The detailed planning project for the second phase of this residential area was approved in 1990 (principal planner: T. Shchehlova). Development of micro-districts No. 4 and No. 5 in the second stage (south of Nahnybida Street) lasted from 1991 to 2006.

11. DAZO, f. P-75, op. 9, spr. 632

pp. 72 – 73

RIGHT BANK

Osypenkivskyi residential area

The first assignment of land for systematic multi-storey development came in 1968: 'Assign a 4.95-hectare plot to the Zaporizhzhia Valve Plant of the USSR Ministry of Chemical and Petroleum Engineering in the western part of the planned residential area on Osypenko Street [since 1970: Talalikhin Street]'.[19] In effect, this was the beginning of the development of the area known as 'micro-district No. 2'. In addition to the valve plant, the clients for this housing development were Zaporizhzhia's Capital Construction Department, a transformer plant, a high-voltage equipment plant, and Dnipro Mechanical Plant. Problems that occurred during the first stage of development (1968–1976) – namely unsatisfactory transport connections and an insufficiency of services enterprises – were solved during planning of the new micro-district (No. 1), construction of which began in 1977.

19. DAZO, f. P-75, op. 6, spr. 312

pp. 40–41

Osypenkivskyi residential area, 1979, photo by P. Ivanenko, from Khortytsia National Reserve Fund

Visual sources

This book uses photographs and graphic material from the following collections and publications (in the case of publications, the number of the book page is given first, followed by a slash sign and the number of the page in the source):

COLLECTIONS

Khortytsia National Reserve: pp. 259, 269

Private collection of Valerii Hushcha, Zaporizhzhia: pp. 8–9, 13, 54–55, 58–59

Richard Nixon Library: pp. 148–149

State Archive of Zaporizhzhia Region (DAZO): p. 86

Zabolotnov State Scientific Library of Architecture and Construction: pp. 60–63, 86, 118, 127, 138–142

Zaporizhzhia Museum of Architecture: pp. 32–33, 68–69, 72–73, 91–92, 97, 100–102, 106–107, 111 114, 122–123, 127, 136–137, 143, 145–147, 153, 172–173, 180–181, 184–187, 190, 192–193, 196, 198–199, 210, 216, 225, 232, 239, 247, 253, 258, 263–268

Zaporizhzhia Regional Organisation of National Union of Architects of Ukraine: pp. 10, 22–24, 26–27, 34–37, 40–47, 70 –71, 74–75, 90, 96, 126, 154–155, 168–169, 182–183, 188–189, 201–207, 212–215, 218–223, 226–231, 235–237, 240–242, 249–251, 254–252, 262.

Zaporizhzhia Regional Organisation of National Union of Photographic Artists of Ukraine: pp. 64–65, 87, 115, 119, 132, 245, 271

PUBLICATIONS

Architecture of Ukraine at a new stage (1954–1964) (Kyiv: Budivelnyk, 1964), p. 12 / 27

Architecture of Ukraine at the modern stage (Kyiv: Budivelnyk, 1984), pp. 110, 194–195 / insert between pp. 32 and 33

Architecture. Works by design and scientific institutes of Moscow, 1975 – 1978 **(**Moscow: Stroiizdat, 1981), pp. 38–39 / 144

*Construction and Architecture***:**
1959, No. 7, pp. 56–57 / insert between pp. 16 and 17
1967. No. 7, pp. 174–179 / 24 –29

Construction. Encyclopaedia of modern technology. Volume 2 (Moscow: Sovetskaya Entsiklopediya, 1964), pp. 52–53 / 81.

Hradov, H., *The city and everyday life (prospects for development of a system and types of public buildings)* (Moscow: Stroiizdat, 1968), pp. 16–17 / 24–25; 18–19 / 148; 134–135 / 20; 152–153 / 213

Ivanova, A., Oriekhova, H., 'New principles of planning and development of the city centre of Zaporizhzhia' in *Bulletin of the Academy of Construction and Architecture of the Ukrainian SSR*, 1960, No. 2, pp. 164–165 / 12–13; 166 / insert between pp. 14 and 15.

New settlement element. On the way to a new city (Moscow: Stroiizdat, 1966), pp. 28–29 / 23; 30–31 / 86

Platonov, H., Pozdniakov, P., *Basics of housing evolution* (Leningrad: Stroiizdat, 1968), pp. 130–131 / 22

Problems of urban planning and development (Chisinau: Tympul, 1969), p. 14 / 49

Problems involved in improving the quality of architecture (Kyiv: Budivelnyk, 1974), pp. 66–67 / 76

Reconstruction and development of large cities in the Ukrainian SSR (Kyiv: Budivelnyk, 1974), pp. 15 / 37; 20–21 / 174

Zaporizhzhia. Photo album (Kyiv: Mystetstvo, 1970), p. 167 / 135

Photo by Dmytro Smolienko, 2024

The *Deutsche Bibliothek* lists this publication in the *Deutsche Nationalbibliografie*; detailed bibliographic data is available on the internet at *http://dnb.d-nb.de*

ISBN 978–3–86922–836-5

Editors
Pavlo Kravchuk
Mykhailo Mordovskoi

Scientific reviewer
Serhii Bilivnenko

Proofreading
John Nicolson

Design
Mykhailo Mordovskoi

Printing
Tiger Printing (Hong Kong) Co., Ltd.
www.tigerprinting.hk

DOM
publishers